SERIES EDITOR: LEE JOHNSON

OSPREY MILITARY MEN-AT-ARMS

ÉMIGRÉ & FOREIGN TROOPS IN BRITISH SERVICE (1) 1793–1802

TEXT BY
RENÉ CHARTRAND

COLOUR PLATES BY
PATRICE COURCELLE

OSPREY
MILITARY

First published in Great Britain in 1999 by Osprey Publishing, Elms Court, Chapel Way, Botley, Oxford OX2 9LP

ISBN 1 85532 766 X

Editor: Martin Windrow
Design: Black Spot
Origination: Valhaven Ltd, Isleworth, UK
Printed through World Print Ltd., Hong Kong

99 00 01 02 03   10 9 8 7 6 5 4 3 2 1

For a catalogue of all books published by Osprey Military, Automotive and Aviation please write to:

The Marketing Manager, Osprey Publishing, P.O. Box 140, Wellingborough, Northants, NN8 4ZA, United Kingdom

OR VISIT OSPREY'S WEBSITE AT: *www.osprey-publishing.co.uk*

Publishers' note

Readers may wish to study this title in conjunction with the following Osprey publications:

MAA 257 *Napoleon's Campaigns in Italy*
MAA 79 *Napoleon's Egyptian Campaign 1798–1801*
MAA 114 *Wellington's Infantry (1)*
MAA 294 *British Forces in the West Indies 1790–1815*

Author's note

The British forces mobilised against Revolutionary and Napoleonic France throughout nearly twenty years of what was virtually a world war from 1793 to 1815 included a number of French Royalist "émigré" units, as well as corps of various other nationalities. As will be seen in this and the forthcoming second volume, a great many of these units served not only in Europe — particularly southern Europe — but also in the West Indies, Africa and Asia. This first book deals with the period from the death of France's King Louis XVI in 1793 to the temporary pause in hostilities following the Peace of Amiens in 1802; the second will trace the story from the resumption of hostilities in 1803 to the final exile of Napoleon in 1815. In a number of cases units listed as disbanded in this volume will be found to have been resurrected in the second.

With regards to the hues of colours described, blue and green were meant to be very dark shades. Red ranged from the brick red of the common soldiers' coats to the fine scarlet of officers' dress. White, especially for waistcoats and breeches, could assume a creamy colour.

Artist's note

Readers may care to note that the original paintings from which the colour plates in this book were prepared are available for private sale. All reproduction copyright whatsoever is retained by the Publishers. All enquiries should be addressed to:

Patrice Courcelle, 38 avenue de Vallons, 1410 Waterloo, Belgium

The Publishers regret that they can enter into no correspondence upon this matter.

ÉMIGRÉ & FOREIGN TROOPS IN BRITISH SERVICE (1) 1793–1802

BRITAIN'S FOREIGN ARMY

Up to the end of the 18th century the British Army did not have a sizeable contingent of foreign soldiers within its establishment. The greatest number served in the 60th (Royal American) Regiment of Foot, which traditionally had a high proportion of Swiss and German personnel, and thus acted as a sort of unofficial foreign corps. The British military establishment held deep-seated prejudices about the reliability of foreign troops, who should, it was felt, be kept at arm's length in far-off garrisons. Furthermore, the laws which prevented Roman Catholics from holding commissioned rank in the Army also excluded many foreign officers.

The tremendous upheavals created by the French Revolution changed all that. From 1789 members of the French nobility were increasingly persecuted, fearing at first for their property and soon for their very lives. Many fled abroad; even the French Royal family finally tried to escape beyond the reach of the Revolution, but were caught at Varennes on 21 June 1791. On 22 September 1792 the monarchy was abolished and France became a republic. After a farcical show trial King Louis XVI was executed on 21 January 1793. The infant French Republic, already fighting Prussia and Austria and scenting a European conspiracy, declared war on Britain and Holland on 1 February 1793.

By that time great numbers of French noble families and non-noble Royalists had already taken refuge in neighbouring countries. They numbered about a quarter of a million souls of both sexes and all ages – almost one per cent of the French population. These exiles became known collectively as the *'émigrés'*.

The execution of the king did not mark the final triumph of the Revolution. Royalist revolts in southern France were surpressed without too much difficulty; but in the west, in southern Brittany and the Vendée, some 40,000 armed peasants under local leaders, provoked both by the anti-clerical stance of the new regime and also by burdensome conscription laws, drove out Republican troops in March 1793. Although the rising – which eventually involved some 65,000

King Louis XVI, Queen Marie-Antoinette and their children anxiously watch with their Life Guards and courtiers as a revolutionary mob invades the Tuilleries palace on 10 August 1792. (Print after E.Brunning)

The persecution of the church by extremist revolutionaries turned many a devout peasant against the Revolution. The *chouan* armies in western France were full of men of deep religious faith who were driven to rebel as much in defence of religion as of the monarchy.

men – was eventually crushed in December 1793, the authority of the Republic was only enforced at an appalling cost. More than 250,000 people perished in battle, in mass executions during a year of savagely ruthless repression, and – in large part – from famine and pestilence. The bitterness engendered by this atrocious civil war was to fester on for many years; there were smaller risings in June 1795 and in 1799, and in such areas stubborn Royalist sympathies endured.

Great Britain at first reacted somewhat slowly to the effects of the French Revolution. While Royalists were fighting for their own communities in the Vendée, and émigrés with the Dutch forces in Flanders,

Armed peasants of the Vendée, c.1793. The insurgents nearly all wore their regional costumes which were often of dark hues. Their weapons included 'cudgels, scythes and reaping hooks' as well as fowling pieces. They disliked knapsacks, and 'preferred to put their cartridges in their pockets' or rolled in a kerchief worn as a waist sash.

Chouans skirmishing with a French Republican battalion formed in square, c.1793–95. The peasants who formed the Royalist armies in the Vendée and Brittany performed well at partisan warfare, but generally could not withstand a pitched battle against regular battalions.

British policy on the subsidising, enlistment or employment of foreign troops was confused. A parliamentary bill 'to enable subjects of France to enlist as soldiers' and receive commissions without suffering 'pain or penalty' for professing 'the Popish Religion' was finally passed in April 1794. This removed the last legal hurdles to raising units. For instance, eight so-called 'white cockade' infantry regiments – each to have 1,657 officers and men in two battalions – were authorised on 1 August 1794; and a 990-man battalion of artillery in November, as well as other corps (PRO, WO 6/5). By that date, however, the numbers of émigré Royalist recruits were dwindling, and some of these regiments could not be raised.

French Republican armies overran Holland at the end of 1794, and British forces present retreated into Hanover. At that point many émigré

A view of the Quiberon peninsula, scene of the émigré and British disaster, seen from the French Republican army's lines after their capture of Fort Penthièvre in August 1795. (Print after Martinet)

and foreign units in Dutch pay were transferred to the British service. In July 1795 came an attempt on the French coast which ended disastrously at Quiberon. This was a catastrophe both for Britain's émigré regiments and for the remaining *chouans* – the insurgents in western France – who were much discouraged despite continuing British aid in arms and money.

By then France had invaded most of its European enemies, forcing them into neutrality or – like Holland and Spain – armed alliance against Great Britain. Many French émigrés in British service, especially officers, dispersed among numerous units in Europe and overseas. German units were partly absorbed into the 60th Foot in 1797–1798. However, in 1799 many Swiss and Dutch units were added so that the foreign establishment remained sizeable. The remnants of the Prince of Condé's army, abandoned by Russia, was subsidised by Britain in northern Italy. In the Vendée organised Royalist forces took up arms again with British material support.

When General Bonaparte took power in France in 1799 he understood the need for a political solution. Freedom of worship was guaranteed, which removed one of the main provocations in the Vendée. Peace between France and Britain finally came in March 1802 – though it would prove short-lived. For the émigrés an amnesty was proclaimed in April 1802: except for those who had served as officers in foreign armies, all others could now return to France, and many did. Great Britain disbanded most of its remaining émigré and foreign corps.

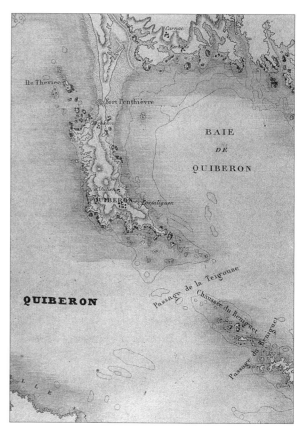

Map of the Quiberon peninsula, 1795.

REGIMENTS AND CORPS 1793–1802

The many units raised between 1793 and 1801 are listed below in alphabetical order, each with a short account of its history and notes on its uniforms, when known. In some cases further information is more logically given in the forthcoming second title on post-1802 activity; or will be found in existing Men-at-Arms titles cited:

Autichamp French émigré 'white cockade' infantry regiment authorised to be raised in Holland from 1.8.1794. Only 189 men enlisted by June 1795; disbanded in Germany on 24.10.1795. *Uniform:* Red coatee; sky blue collar, cuffs, turnbacks, shoulder straps; white piping, pewter buttons stamped '3'; white waistcoat and breeches, black gaiters; black round hat with bearskin crest, red turban, white cockade, loop and plume. Silver buttons and epaulettes for officers.

Bachmann Two-battalion regiment raised from 14.7.1799 in St.Gall Canton, Switzerland; commanded by Baron Nicolas Bachmann, an experienced officer who had served in France and Piedmont. 1st Bn fought at Zurich with Russians against French, 25–26.9.1799, losing some 500 men in subsequent retreat. Deployed on the southern Rhine and saw much fighting in July 1800; courageous behaviour noted at battle of Feldkirsch (13 July). Attacked French at Ponte and Campovasto (8 December), capturing over 360 officers and men and colour of the 3rd Orient Half-Brigade. Austro-Swiss units, including Bachmann's, had to retreat before superior French forces in late December and went into Austria in January 1801. An armistice was signed; the British assembled the Swiss corps in their service at Mahrburg, where Bachmann's was disbanded on 4.5.1801. On 23 May four officers and 118 men joined Watteville (qv).

Uniform: Initially, Austrian-style sky blue coat with black collar, cuffs and turnbacks, brass buttons; sky blue waistcoat and breeches, black half-gaiters; black felt cap with brass oval frontal plate bearing 'B', black plume at left; white accoutrements. The second uniform worn from early 1800 was a green coatee; red collar, cuffs and turnbacks, brass buttons; sky blue pantaloons, black half-gaiters; black shako with black turban, brass oval plate with 'B', yellow plume tipped black, green oakleaf; white accoutrements.

Béon Raised in Dutch service from 4.3.1793 with six companies of chasseurs; two companies of hussars added from 25.5.1793; company establishment 115 all ranks. Saw much fighting against the French Republicans during 1793–94; infantry evacuated from Holland to Hanover and taken into British service from 9.2.1795. There were then 137 hussars and 134 infantry of all ranks. The infantry were sent to England; arriving in Portsmouth on 2 July, they sailed on 9 July for Quiberon. About 250 infantry landed on 17 July but were caught in the disastrous battle of the 21st; only 38 officers and men returned, being drafted into Loyal Emigrant (qv) on 8 October. The hussars, who had remained in Germany, were disbanded on either 24.12.1795 or 15.6.1796.

Uniform: Fusiliers Sky blue coat; orange collar, cuffs and lapels, white turnbacks, pewter buttons; white waistcoat, sky blue breeches, black half-gaiters; hat with white plume, black accoutrements. *Chasseurs* Coatee closed in front, in same colours but with facings edged yellow and sky blue collar; round hat with brim turned up at left and white plume. *Hussars* Sky blue dolman, pelisse and breeches; orange dolman collar and cuffs, black fur trim on pelisse, white cords and lace, pewter buttons; sky blue visorless shako with white cords and plume; white and orange sash, sky blue sabretache edged white with white crowned 'GR'. (Many variations noted.)

Béthisy French émigré 'white cockade' infantry regiment authorised raised in Holland from 1.8.1794. Only 104 men by June 1795; ordered suspended in July, and disbanded in Germany 24.10.1795, most joining Condé's Army. *Uniform:* See accompanying illustration.

Broderick To be raised from Albanians during 1799, along with Villettes regiment (qv). Field officers appointed from 12.4.1799; CO Lt.Col.Broderick, late 1st Foot Guards. Some recruits assembled on Corfu late in year, but the scheme was abandoned. *Uniform:* Red jacket, green collar and cuffs, white buttonhole loops, pewter buttons, white breeches (C.Hamilton Smith MS).

Broglie French émigré 'white cockade' infantry regiment raised in Holland from 11.10.1794; Broglie's commission back-dated to 1 August

Count Joseph de Puisaye (1755–1827) was one of the most controversial chiefs of the Émigrés. He advocated a landing in France which would result in a general revolt of Vendéens. The Quiberon disaster, where he fought bravely and managed to escape, destroyed his later influence as much of the blame for failure was laid on him – although this seems, in retrospect, unjust. He went to Canada with about 40 Royalists in 1798 to establish a military colony of Royalist veterans at Niagara; after this scheme failed Puisaye travelled to England late in 1801. He was not allowed back into France after the return of Louis XVIII, and died at Blythe House near Hammersmith, London.

(PRO, WO 4/154). Retreated into Hanover in early 1795; only 230 officers and men recruited by June; disbanded 24.10.1795. *Uniform:* See Plate A.

Cadres Corps These corps were made up of former officers of the French Royal army. The infantry regiments were organised by recruiting gentlemen who were to become officers of the Royalist insurgents in the event of a landing in France. Each infantry cadre unit had an establishment of 319 gentlemen who held double rank: e.g., the four captains in the cadre regiment would rank as colonels in France, the 29 corporals would be captains, etc.:–

– **Léon** Raised from 5.12.1794 on Jersey by Alexandre de Rohan-Chabot, Prince of Léon, with Breton gentlemen; three companies were to be formed of volunteers from Dresnay's corps (PRO, WO

Béthisy's Regiment, 1794–95. Red coatee, bright yellow collar, cuffs, turnbacks, shoulder straps; white piping, pewter buttons stamped with '5'; white waistcoat and breeches, black gaiters; black round hat with bearskin crest and red turban, white cockade, loop and plume. Silver buttons and epaulettes for officers. (Anne S.K.Brown Military Collection, Brown University, Providence. Photo R.Chartrand)

LEFT **Bouillé's Uhlans Britanniques, c.1793–95.** White lancer cap with black fur turban, yellow cords, red plume; red jacket with green collar, cuffs and turnbacks, yellow braid (criss-crossed on the breast), brass buttons; green waistcoat and breeches laced yellow; green housings and valise edged red; white sheepskin, yellow and red quartered lance pennant. (Anne S.K.Brown Military Collection, Brown University, Providence. Photo R.Chartrand)

1/617); 307 strong by April 1795. Sent to Isle d'Yeu in September, to Jersey in November, to Southampton in August 1796; disbanded at Ryde, 7.11.1796. *Uniform:* Green coat and breeches.

— **Trésor** Formed from 5.12.1794 on Jersey by Comte Louis du Trésor de Bactot with volunteers from Brittany and Normandy; three companies were to be formed of volunteers from Dresnay's (qv) corps (PRO, WO 1/617); 250-plus officers and men by April 1795. Was to land at Quiberon but sent back to Jersey, then to England in August 1796; disbanded at Ryde on 7.11.1796. *Uniform:* Green, silver epaulettes and sword knots.

— **Williamson** Formed from 2.3.1795 in Guernsey (by the Comte Oiliamson, who had anglicised his name) with nearly 300 Norman gentlemen. About 40 volunteers landed at Quiberon in June and eventually officered *chouan* bands; 60 more landed in Normandy in December. On Jersey until sent to England in August 1796; disbanded at Ryde, 7.11.1796. *Uniform:* Reversible green and grey jackets.

— **Allonville** Raised from 1.5.1795 among French émigrés in Germany, commanded by Comte Armand d'Allonville. Left Bremen about 300 strong in August; on Guernsey until August 1796 when transferred to England; disbanded 7.11.1796. *Uniform:* Grey with white sash, buttons stamped with three fleurs-de-lis.

— **Quiefdeville Artillery Cadres** Some French Royalist artillery officers under Lt.Col.François-Charles de Quiefdeville were taken into British pay at Portsmouth in January 1794; about 66 were sent into Flanders that May. Most passed into Rotalier's artillery (qv) in May 1795; others in England were released from service in January 1795. *Uniform:* Apparently same as French Corps Royal de l'Artillerie.

— **Engineer Officer Cadres** Some French engineer officers assembled in England from September 1793 and at Ostend in December; taken into British pay, assembled on the Isle of Wight in early 1794; about 15 served in Flanders. Others were formed into a 16-officer 'brigade' from April 1795 which took part in Quiberon expedition; went to Portugal 1797–1802. Others fought in capture of Majorca, served in Egypt and West Indies. *Uniform:* Probably same as French Corps Royal du Génie.

Cape Corps Following Britain's capture of Cape of Good Hope, South Africa, from Dutch in 1795, the need for a local unit was soon felt, and this was raised in 1797 under Lt.J.Campbell, 98th Foot. Some 500–600 strong, it was recruited from mixed blood Hottentots previously in Dutch service; a few were mounted and acted as orderlies. Taken into Dutch service as 'Hottentot Light Infantry' when the colony was returned to Holland in 1802. *Uniform:* Blue jacket with red facings, pewter buttons; Indian-style breeches ending above the knees; round hat.

Carneville Authorised raised in Germany by the Vicomte de Carneville from 2.2.1795, but he failed to recruit the promised four hussar squadrons and six light infantry companies; those who had enlisted were transferred to other units from 25 May.

Castries French émigré 'white cockade' infantry regiment raised in Holland from 1.8.1794. Over 350 strong by June 1795; evacuated from Germany to England in November 1795. Reorganised into ten-company single-battalion regiment with additional company of Chasseurs Nobles in January 1796. Embarked for Portugal, January 1797, numbering 751 all ranks including Chasseur Nobles. The regiment remained on the Spanish border but was not engaged. Chasseurs Nobles sent back to England, July 1801, and incorporated into Foreign Invalids (qv); rest of regiment in Portugal until August 1802, when sent to England; disbanded at Portsmouth.

Uniform 1794: Red coatee, light green collar, cuffs, turnbacks and shoulder straps, white piping, pewter buttons stamped '8'; white waistcoat and breeches, black gaiters; black round hat, bearskin crest and red turban, white cockade, loop and plume. *From 1797:* See Plate H.

Choiseul's Hussars, 1794–96. Green dolman with scarlet collar and cuffs, mixed yellow and red cords, brass buttons; green pelisse with yellow and red cords and brass buttons, white fur trim; buff breeches trimmed with yellow and red lace, yellow and crimson barrel sash, black hussar boots edged with yellow and red cord; black shako with yellow bands, black cockade edged yellow, yellow loop and cords, white plume; red sabretache with yellow edging and crowned 'GR'; black cartridge box belt, buff sabre belt; green housings edged red, white sheepskin; armed with sabre and carbine. (Anne S.K.Brown Military Collection, Brown University, Providence. Photo R.Chartrand)

Ceylon Regiments Following British capture of Ceylon (now Sri Lanka) in 1796, former Dutch garrison largely incorporated into British forces. Independent companies of Malays in Dutch service were formed into a regiment under the Honourable East India Company for service in Ceylon; but five of its companies were sent to India, 1799, seeing action on the Malabar coast. Regiment transferred to British establishment, 1801, under command of Col.J.Champagné; became 1st Ceylon Regiment in 1802 when a 2nd Ceylon Regiment was recruited from Singhalese by Col.W.Ramsay.

Uniform: Red British infantry coatee, white lace, pewter buttons; white breeches. Bicorns or perhaps round hats until c.1801–1802, then stovepipe shakos; 2nd Ceylon asked for blue turbans instead in 1802. Facings for 1st Regt were white (C.Hamilton Smith MS chart under 'Champagnie') or buff; 2nd Regt, light green; gold buttons and lace for officers of both regiments. (See also Vol.2)

Chasseurs Britanniques Formed from May 1801 from remnants of Condé's Army following Peace of Luneville – concluded February 1801 between France and most European powers, but not Britain – under Col.John Ramsay, former Inspector General of Foreign Corps. Regiment to serve only in Europe and the Mediterranean, forming light infantry battalion of six companies mustering about 600 men. Besides French émigrés many Germans, Poles and Swiss enlisted, but officers remained French. Embarked from Trieste, arriving Malta in early June, Egypt in August 1801 as reinforcements at Alexandria. Saw little action; back in Malta by December 1801, remaining until 1803.

Uniform: Green coatee with black or yellow collar, black half-lapels, pointed cuffs, shoulder straps and turnbacks, pewter buttons; grey long breeches, black half-gaiters; cylindrical shako, white metal bugle horn badge, black cockade, green plume; black accoutrements; some apparently armed with German rifles. (See also Vol.2)

Chasseurs Britanniques de Saint-Domingue (Montalembert's) See MAA 294 *British Forces in the West Indies 1793–1815.*

Choiseul's Hussars Six hussar companies each of 135 all ranks, and one horse artillery company of 35; raised by Claude-Antoine, Duc de Choiseul-Stainville at Courtrai from 15.3.1794. It had 19 officers and 653 men in August but lacked horses, part of the regiment serving on foot. Many engagements against French Republicans along the Bommel and Meuse rivers in autumn 1794; in Holland by December with 400 sick and 350 fit for service; retreated into Hanover early in 1795. The corps's first division of 550 men sailed for England, August 1795; sent on to Quiberon on 11 September; on to Ile d'Yeu; and finally back in England, near Southampton, by late November. Most of the rest of the corps in Germany sailed for India in September, but their ships were wrecked in the Channel off Calais and they were made prisoner. Their release was obtained by the British government on the pretext that they were of the Indian Army, most reaching Portsmouth in December. The two detachments of Choiseul were reunited on the Isle of Wight in January 1796, about 550 strong; but disbanded in early March 1796.

Uniform: See illustration for hussars. *Artillery company* Green coatee and breeches; scarlet collar, pointed cuffs, turnbacks, shoulder straps, wings and waistcoat, yellow and red cords, brass buttons; round hat with fur crest, green turban and plume in 1793, replaced 1795 by Tarleton helmet with red turban, yellow ribbon at back, white plume. Officers had gold buttons, cords and lace including gold-edged housings.

Corsican Chasseurs Also known as Corsican French Chasseurs and MacLean's Chasseurs. First company formed at Toulon on 31.10.1793, second on 6.11.1793, each 100 strong. Gave good service during the siege and evacuated by British fleet which went on to take Corsica, where both companies left in garrison. Transferred to Elba, October 1796; to Portugal, June 1797 and reduced to one company. Disbanded on 24.6.1798 and men drafted into Loyal Emigrant (qv).

Corsican Gendarmerie Also called Corps royal de la Gendarmerie or Royal Anglo-Corsican Gendarmerie; constabulary unit organised from February 1794 in four companies of 50 men each from former French Republican gendarmes. Augmented by 400 men forming eight new companies in early 1796. Mostly employed against 'rebels' (bandits) in mountainous interior. The four original companies changed from British to French service following British evacuation in October 1796. *Uniform:* Probably as French Gendarmerie, but with black cockade.

Corsican Light Dragoons Two companies of three officers and 35 men each raised from November 1794 in Corsica; found to be of little use, and disbanded from September 1795.

Corsican Rangers Raised in Minorca from 25.6.1799 with refugees from Corsica and emigrés, completed to seven officers and 226 men by October. First commander Capt.Masseria, succeeded on 1.7.1800 by Maj.Hudson Lowe. October 1800, sent to Gibraltar where Gen.Abercromby's army was assembling for Egypt – where Corsican Rangers landed under fire on 8.3.1801 with Gen.Moore's Reserve Brigade. Earned excellent reputation on outpost duty and skirmishing with enemy until 13 August, when British besieged Alexandria. Transferred to Malta in January 1802; disbanded there on 1 July following Treaty of Amiens.

Damas' Hussars, 1793–96. Sky blue dolman and breeches, black collar and cuffs; ash grey pelisse trimmed with black fur, mixed white and black cords and lace, pewter buttons; crimson and white sash; black shako with white lace and cords, black plume; sky blue sabretache edged white with crowned 'GR' and later, with Condé's army, white fleur-de-lis. (Anne S.K.Brown Military Collection, Brown University, Providence. Photo R.Chartrand)

OPPOSITE **Damas' Infantry, 1793–95.** Sky blue coat, black collar piped white, red collar tab piped white, black cuffs and lapels piped white; white pointed loops at the lapels, one on the cuff and one above set horizontally; white turnbacks, pewter buttons; white waistcoat and breeches; hat with black (white at Quiberon) cockade and white loop; white accoutrements. (Anne S.K.Brown Military Collection, Brown University, Providence. Photo R.Chartrand)

Uniform: Two different uniforms are given for this unit. According to Charles Hamilton Smith's MS chart, c.1799–1800 they had a red coatee, yellow collar and cuffs, white buttonhole lace for the men – possibly the first uniform worn in Minorca. See Plate G for the uniform in Egypt.

Corsican Regiment (also called Union Regiment of Foot or Smith's Regiment). Raised in Corsica from 4.4.1795, commanded by Maj.George Smith, to have five companies each of 130 men with mostly British officers but a few Corsican subalterns; 675 all ranks on strength by September. The regiment basically dissolved when the British prepared to evacuate the island in November 1796, the men deserting and the Corsican officers resigning their commissions on the 24th. *Uniform:* Red coat, yellow collar, cuffs and turnbacks, pewter buttons; white waistcoat and breeches; bicorn hat with white plume.

Courten Raised from 14.6.1799 in Switzerland by Comte Antoine de Courten, authorised to raise only three companies totalling 144 all ranks by December. Moved to Torino, Italy; apparently served with Austro-Piedmontese at battle of Marengo; escaped French besieging Verona, early February 1800, and returned to Switzerland. Four officers and 189 enlisted men joined Watteville's (qv) on 23.5.1801.

Uniform: Green coatee with yellow collar, cuffs and turnbacks, brass buttons; green waistcoat with two rows of brass buttons; sky blue Hungarian-style long breeches, black half-gaiters; black shako with black turban edged yellow, black cockade with yellow loop, green oakleaf above; white accoutrements.

Damas Raised in Dutch service from 25.5.1793 by Comte Étienne-Charles de Damas-Crux, the Legion of Damas saw much action against the French. Retreated into Hanover; passed into British service 22.2.1795, with 660-plus all ranks in two companies of hussars (or mounted chasseurs), two of foot chasseurs and four of fusiliers. Predominantly French émigrés, many being ex-officers. Some 300 infantry sent to Plymouth and on to Quiberon, landing 17 July; nearly all lost in disastrous engagement on the 21st – only 14 escaped, to be incorporated into Loyal Emigrant (qv) on 8 October. The cavalry, 240 strong, remained in Germany; although disbanded on paper in December 1795, Damas' Hussars continued to be paid by Britain. They evacuated Hanover, attaching themselves to the Prince of Condé's army in March 1796 some 370 strong, and fought bravely against Gen.Moreau's French in many engagements in the Rhineland, 1796–97. From 1.10.1797 Condé's army was taken into Russian pay, and Damas' Hussars were disbanded. *Uniform:* See illustrations.

(Edward) Dillon's Regiment Authorised raised in northern Italy from 1.2.1795 by Col.Edward Dillon, formerly of the Irish Brigade of the French Royal army. Only its original Lt.Col.Francis Dillon and Maj.Doran were of Irish ancestry, most other officers being French émigrés. Initially the men were largely French and Italian but, from 1796, increasing numbers from Germany and the Balkans were enlisted.

Damas' Chasseurs, 1793–95. Sky blue coatee, black piped white collar with red piped white collar tab, black piped white cuffs and lapels, white pointed buttonhole lace at the lapels and one on the cuff and one above set horizontally, pewter buttons, sky blue breeches, round hat with left brim turned up, white lace edging brim and round the crown, white tipped black plume, black accoutrements. (Anne S.K.Brown Military Collection, Brown University, Providence. Photo R. Chartrand)

Dillon roamed across northern Italy until it went to Corsica in April 1796; formed two battalions each 750 strong; moved to Elba in December, and to Portugal in June 1797. From August 1799 to March 1801 at Port Mahon, Minorca; landed in Egypt, and fought with distinction on 13.3 and 21.3.1801. Garrisoned Alexandria and Cairo until sent to Malta in early 1803. (See also Vol.2)

Uniform: Initially red coatee with yellow collar, cuffs and half-lapels, white turnbacks, pewter buttons; white waistcoat and breeches; hat with short white-over-red plume. From 1800–1802, stovepipe shako; coatee without lapels but with white lace with grey line in bastion-shape loops set evenly. Silver buttons and lace for officers.

(Henry) Dillon's Regiment Served in Haiti 1793–96; see MAA 294 *British Forces in the West Indies 1793–1815.*

Dresnay Officially authorised on 1.8.1794 as 'white cockade' regiment, but over 500 men of Dresnay's Legion were already on Jersey in late 1793; recruited up to 700, and destined for Quiberon expedition. Officers were largely Bretons who had held Royal commissions; but men included some untrustworthy French Republican deserters and former prisoners. Landing at Quiberon in July 1795, the regiment was practically wiped out, some of the men killing their officers and joining the Republicans. About 40 captured officers were executed by firing squad; only eight officers and 37 men escaped; unit disbanded 24.10.1795.

Uniform: Red coatee, dark green collar, cuffs, turnbacks and shoulder straps, white piping, pewter buttons stamped '9'; white waistcoat and breeches, black gaiters; black round hat with bearskin crest and red turban, white cockade, loop and plume. Officers had silver buttons and epaulettes.

Dutch Emigrant Artillery Initially raised in Hanover, 1795, with about 200 Dutch artillerymen. First company embodied from 29 March under Capt.Nacquard (later major and commanding officer), a second in August and a third in October, with four officers and 107 men each, plus six staff. Transferred to England in second half of 1795, and sent to Haiti in April 1796. See MAA 294 *British Forces in the West Indies 1793–1815.*

Dutch Emigrant Brigade Some 3,000 Dutch soldiers evacuated to Britain, autumn 1799; organised into brigade on Isle of Wight – four infantry regiments each with attached artillery company, and pioneer battalion including one engineer company. November 1800, artillery companies detached to form battalion, also incorporating engineer company. The eight regimental light companies were grouped in two light infantry battalions. Further Dutch refugees brought strength well over 4,000; battalions had 41 officers and 812 other ranks – except light infantry battalions, each with 20 officers and 434 men each (these inlcuded rifle companies). Except for brief service in southern Ireland, 1801, they remained in the Channel Islands until disbanded in 1802 following Peace of Amiens, most personnel returning to Holland.

Uniform: Infantry & Light Infantry Blue British-style coatee, red collar and cuffs, white turnbacks, white square-ended loops set equally with narrow red centre, pewter buttons, grey breeches; bicorn hats, replaced by stovepipe shakos with brass plates from 1800, white plume. *Artillery & Pioneers* The same but with black collar and cuffs. *Rifle Companies* Green coatee, black collar, cuffs, lapels and turnbacks, brass buttons; grey breeches; black shako with brass bugle horn, green cords, green-over-white tuft; black rifle accoutrements.

Dutch West Indies & Surinam colonial troops Most were amalgamated or continued to serve with the British forces. See MAA 294 *British Forces in the West Indies 1793–1815.*

Emigrant Corps of Saint Domingue (Haiti) *Compagnies franches d'Émigrés* organised from December 1795 for local protection; originally the *Gardes Soldées de la Grande Anse* (Paid Guards of Grande Anse) in south-west Haiti, they could now be formed all over the colony, apparently recruiting Royalist white colonists rather than émigrés from France. Company establishment, 56 all ranks (PRO, T81/14). They vanished with the British withdrawal in 1798.

Erlacht On 6.4.1796 Comte Victor d'Erlacht undertook to raise a ten-company infantry battalion in Switzerland within four months. He failed, due to the Swiss cantons' fear of provoking the French. The uniform was to have been red with black lapels.

Foreign Engineers & Artificers Company of 93 men raised in Corsica, 1794, but disbanded on British evacuation in October 1796.

Foreign Invalids Independent Companies One company raised on Isle of Wight, late 1798, second in Lymington from 25.7.1801, with veterans from Loyal Emigrant, Castries and Mortemat's regiments (qqqv). (See also Vol.2)

Franco-Maltese Artillery Company See Maltese Artillery Company.

French (Black) Chasseurs Company formed by Governor of Jamaica, late 1798, with refugee black Chasseurs from Haiti led by white French Émigré officers. Sent to Honduras, and eventually incorporated into 6th West India Regiment stationed there (PRO, WO1/770). *Uniform:* Probably as the Black Chasseurs on Haiti – red jacket, white pantaloons and round hat.

Gendarmes Royaux Anglais (Haiti) Proposed by Marquis de Contades and approved by Gen.Williamson, Governor General of San Domingo (Haiti) on 10.8.1794, it was intended to serve in British-occupied parts of Haiti, and was raised there from autumn 1794. Establishment was 240 infantry in four 60-man companies, a company of 60

Guides à cheval, c.1794. Red coat, blue collar and cuffs, white turnbacks, pewter buttons; white waistcoat and breeches, black round hat edged white with black cockade and white plume; red valise. (Anne S.K.Brown Military Collection, Brown University, Providence. Photo R.Chartrand)

RIGHT **Francis de Rottenburg, a Polish-born officer who served in Hompesch's Chasseurs before transferring to the 60th Foot in 1797, was one of the most innovative light infantry tactical experts of his day. He is shown in tho officer's uniform of the Line infantry battalions of the 60th Foot, Royal Americans: scarlet coat faced blue with silver buttons and lace. (Print after miniature)**

RIGHT **Hervilly's Regiment, 1794–95. Red coatee, buff collar, cuffs, turnbacks and shoulder straps, white piping, pewter buttons stamped '10'; white waistcoat and breeches, black gaiters; black round hat with bearskin crest and red turban, white cockade, loop and plume. Officers had silver buttons and epaulettes. (Anne S.K.Brown Military Collection, Brown University, Providence. Photo R.Chartrand)**

artillerymen, and 300 cavalry in five 60-man companies. Companies each had three officers; the colonel commandant, de Contades, was assisted by two colonels, two lieutenant-colonels and two majors – double the usual proportion of field officers; the pay scale approved by Williamson was also higher than the usual British norm. All officers had served in the French Royal army; rankers were mostly Royalist white settlers. Recruiting proved difficult; in December 1795 the corps, posted at the fortress town of Môle Saint-Nicolas, mustered only 225 enlisted men with some of the cavalry companies having no troopers at all. Eventually the pay scale was brought down to British levels and the number of field officers was reduced. Aparently not deployed in any major campaign and used as a guard unit at Môle Saint-Nicolas, the corps avoided the major reorganisations which eliminated many other units. It may have increased to about 400 white officers and men with 40 black auxiliaries by the time it was evacuated to Jamaica, where it was disbanded in late 1798. *Uniform:* See Plate E.

Guernsey Hussars Unit about 100 strong formed on Guernsey, October 1797, from men of Rohan's and Hompesch's (qqv) left behind or survivors from Haiti. Incorporated into York Hussars (qv), February 1800.

Hector's Royal Marine (also called Régiment d'Hector). Raised in Southampton area from 1.10.1794 by Comte Jean-Claude d'Hector, nearly all officers and many men being from French Royal navy. Some 700 men by June 1795 – five fusilier companies, two of grenadiers and one of officers. Landed at Carnac, Brittany, on 27 June with other émigré units and went on to Quiberon. On 16 July it suffered 228 casualties out of 440 in fierce fighting; on 21st, another 200 lost at Fort Penthièvre. Only 41 officers and 74 rankers escaped; disbanded 24.10.1795. *Uniform:* See Plate D.

Hervilly 'White cockade' regiment raised from 1.8.1794 by Louis-Charles Le Cat, Comte d'Hervilly; depot at Lindhurst, Hampshire, and recruiting centre at Kaiserwerth near Dusseldorf, Germany. By December, due to incorporation of refugees from Toulon, Royal Louis Regiment (qv), and some recruits from Germany, strength stood at 93 officers and 866 men; later French POWs were recruited. 80 officers and 1,238 men landed at Carnac on 27 June, to Fort Penthièvre on 2 July where some 300 Republican prisoners were incorporated. It fought valiantly on 7, 11 and 16 July, though 33 men deserted to the Republicans on the 19th. Guided by some of Hervilly's deserters, 300 grenadiers of Gen.Hoche's Republican troops got inside the Royalist position and raised the tricolour. Hervilly's 2nd Bn came up but, at the sight of the Republicans, the men turned about and fired on their own officers. Others rallied around the colours but the behaviour of the

Hompesch's Hussars, c.1795. Green dolman with scarlet collar and cuffs, green pelisse trimmed with black fur, white cords, pewter buttons; crimson and white sash, scarlet breeches laced white; black boots trimmed white; scarlet shako with white band, cords and plume, black cockade edged white, white loop; scarlet sabretache trimmed with white; green housings edged scarlet, piped white on the inside; green valise edged scarlet. Armed with sabre and carbine; black accoutrements. The officers had silver buttons, cords and lace; it was said that officers' buttons bore the Prince of Wales's three plumes and motto 'Ich Dien' in 1796. (Anne S.K.Brown Military Collection, Brown University, Providence. Photo R.Chartrand)

recently enlisted turncoats had disastrous results. Some 30 officers and 177 men escaped; 22 captured officers were executed. On 25 October the regiment was disbanded. Hervilly himself, badly wounded on 16 July, was evacuated to London where he died of wounds on 14 November. *Uniform:* See illustration.

Hompesch's Hussars Raised by Baron Charles Hompesch at Schwarm, Hanover, from 27.2.1794, to consist of three squadrons each of three troops, each of three officers and 81 men. Officers were mostly former French Royal army, the men being Germans, Hungarians and émigrés. Joined British forces in Holland during August; fought at Boxtel, 15.9.1794, losing about 30 men. Desertions took strength about 400 below establishment. Evacuated to Hanover in January 1795; augmented by a squadron and ordered completed in April 1795, the regiment was shipped to England in December. It was up to nearly 1,100 when it was inspected that month on the Isle of Wight by the Prince of Wales who – favourably impressed – granted the title 'Prince of Wales's (Hompesch's) Hussars'. Sent to Haiti in March 1796; although engaged in several skirmishes, it lost 90% of its officers and men to disease, and ceased to exist as a corps by October 1797. The remnants were sent back to England. *Uniform:* See illustration.

Hompesch's Chasseurs Raised in Hanover at same time as Hompesch's Hussars, to consist of two companies each of 105 all ranks; officers largely from (German) La Mark Regiment of French Royal army and men

German, Austrian and Dutch. Joined Duke of York's army at Breda in August and deployed as skirmishers. At Boxtel, 13.9.94, lost three-quarters of those engaged, and more in subsequent retreat; less than 120 survivors. Retreated into Hanover with British forces, January 1795, and disbanded at Bergen in early April. *Uniform:* See illustration, and Plate B.

Hompesch's Light Infantry (also occasionally called Hompesch's Fusiliers, or Hompesch's Chasseurs like previous unit.) Recruited in Germany by Baron Charles' younger brother Ferdinand, from 3.3.1796, to consist of eight companies of four officers and 115 men each. Supposed to carry carbines with rifles for ten men per company. Assembled on Isle of Wight as ten-company regiment with some 1,150 men by October 1796; divided into 450 chasseurs armed with rifles and 690 fusiliers, and sailed for West Indies at end of year. Reported 33 officers and 900 men on Martinique, 1.2.1797; participated in capture of Trinidad on 15 February, where left in garrison until November when sent to Antigua, much reduced by disease. On 1.5.1798 its 545 officers and men were incorporated into 60th Foot, chasseurs into 2nd Bn and fusiliers into new 5th Rifle Battalion. *Uniform:* See illustration of shako plate.

Hompesch's Mounted Rifles (also called Hompesch Light Dragoons). Three companies of Mounted Chasseurs, raised by Ferdinand de Hompesch from September 1796 and posted on Isle of Wight, formed basis of new corps 'Hompesch's Mounted Rifles' from 9.1.1798. Recruits were German, in four troops of 114 men each. Sent to Ireland from April; engaged against Irish rebels at Wexford in June; took part in pursuit of small French force helping the Irish in August, earning a savage reputation. In July 1800, 164 officers and men sent from Ireland to participate in abortive raids on Ferrol and Cadiz in Spain, then on to Egypt until sent back to rejoin regiment at Cork, Ireland, in mid-1802. The unit, 450 strong, was transferred to Portsmouth, and disbanded 28.9.1802. *Uniform:* See Plate G.

Irish Catholic Brigade It may seem odd to class these regiments, recruited in Ireland, as émigrés or foreigners; but they were not really seen as an integral part of the British Army. During 1794 the notion of transferring officers of the old French Royal army's Irish Brigade into British service and rec-ruiting enlisted men for their regiments amongst Irish Catholics was considered by British ministers. There was, however, much opposition from the Protestant Irish, who did not

ABOVE **Hompesch's Chasseurs, 1794–1795. This does not show some of the listed features; the green coatee faced and turned-back with scarlet was supposedly piped white and had pointed cuffs; pewter buttons, white waistcoat, green breeches, black half-gaiters; round hat with black bearskin crest, scarlet turban, green plume and plain brim edge are evident, but not the white cockade loop. The unit had black accoutrements and was armed with rifles. (Anne S.K.Brown Military Collection, Brown University, Providence. Photo R.Chartrand)**

LEFT **Sketch of a shako plate of Hompesch's Light Infantry, 1797–98, found on Antigua. The uniform was a green jacket with red collar, pointed cuffs, lapels, shoulder straps and turnbacks and pewter buttons; sky blue pantaloons piped red, black half-gaiters; and a black cylindrical shako with the brass plate shown, yellow band and red turban, black cockade and green plume. The unit was armed with rifles with sword-bayonets or carbines with bayonets and hangers, and was issued black accoutrements.**

wish to see 'Papists' granted military rights. William Pitt the Younger prevailed, and several French-Irish officers were invited to form corps from October 1794; but the actual formation of the brigade met with considerable difficulties, due both to Protestant hostility and lack of Catholic enthusiasm, and financial and bureaucratic problems. There were to be six regiments: Duke of Fitz-James, Count Walsh, Hon.H.Dillon, Count Daniel O'Connell, Viscount Walsh, Count Conway. There were soon amalgamations and changes. In January 1796 Conway died and his unit was amalgamated into Walsh; in March, Fitz-James was amalgamated into other units. The four remaining regiments were ordered amalgamated into two in April 1797, but this could not be carried out as they had already left for America. They service was, briefly, as follows:

Count Walsh's sailed 21.11.1796 for West Indies; sickness broke out on board, and 246 sick were landed in Barbados, 100 in Martinique, besides 36 died during the passage. At Martinique, February-July, then to Port Royal, Jamaica. Three companies detached to Honduras (Belize), September 1797–June 1798, when remnants returned to England. Seven other companies were sent to Haiti, serving there until evacuated in August 1798; in England by late October or November, and disbanded at Chatham.

Dillon's shipped to West Indies from March 1796. (This regiment, led by Col.the Hon.H.Dillon, should not be confused with Edward Dillon's Regiment raised in northern Italy during 1795, nor with Dillon's Regiment in Haiti which came into British service from 1793 – qqv.) Served in Jamaica until autumn 1796 when sent to Haiti, where some 20 black pioneers were added to the strength. Participated in several actions, notably assault on Fort Guérin, 16–17.4.1797. Evacuated from Port au Prince in June 1798, the remnants disbanded on arrival in England.

Viscount Walsh's went to Jamaica in March 1796, adding 20 black pioneers in September. April 1797 sent to Halifax, Nova Scotia; October, returned to England, and disbanded at Chatham 25.12.1797.

Conway's was to sail from Passage near Waterford, Ireland, for Nova Scotia in June 1797, but sickness broke out on board and many sick were left on Spike Island before the convoy finally sailed in October. Detachment posted in Halifax from November 1797, more following in early 1798. Sent back to England in September 1798 and disbanded.

The whole experiment of the Irish Catholic Brigade ended with orders to disband it from Christmas Day 1797. Because some units were overseas this process carried over into 1798 and even 1799 as detachments came back to England. Some sources give the regiments as numbered from 1st to 6th in 1795: 1st Fitz-James, 2nd Count Walsh, 3rd Dillon, 4th O'Connell, 5th Viscount Walsh, 6th Conway. Later Dillon is given as the 1st, while Count Conway's is 3rd and Walsh 4th as late as November 1796 in the returns, so there was some confusion even during the short existence of these units.

Uniform: Red coat with collar, cuffs and lapels of the facing colour, white turnbacks, white lace, pewter buttons; white waistcoat and breeches; bicorn; white accoutrements. Facings are known only for two regiments: blue or sky blue with silver officer's lace for O'Connell's; yellow for the '3rd Regt.Irish Brigade', according to a surviving regimental colour.

Lowenstein's Chasseurs, c.1794–95. Black round hat with yellow cockade loop on the up-turned side and a green plume; blue-grey or dark sky blue coatee with green collar, cuffs, lapels and turnbacks, brass buttons; white (later green) breeches, black gaiters, black accoutrements; armed with rifles with sword-bayonets. (Anne S.K.Brown Military Collection, Brown University, Providence. Photo R.Chartrand)

Loyal Emigrant Regiment, 1793–97. Red coat with yellow collar, cuffs, lapels and shoulder straps, white turnbacks, white square loops with red and black or red and yellow lines, pewter buttons with 'Loyal Emigrant'; white waistcoat and breeches, black gaiters; hat laced white with white tuft and black cockade; white accoutrements. (Anne S.K.Brown Military Collection, Brown University, Providence. Photo R.Chartrand)

La Trémoïlle Infantry regiment raised in Germany from 7.5.1795 by Prince Louis de La Trémoïlle. Several hundred men were recruited but, owing to various misadventures, the regiment could not be formed.

Loewenstein's Chasseurs Raised in Germany for the Dutch service by Prince Charles de Loewenstein from 19.5.1794; reported at Maestricht in August and in action from December. Retreated into Hanover, March 1795, and taken into British pay late April, when of seven companies; augmented to two battalions each of six 100-strong companies. Transferred to Portsmouth in November; part was immediately sent to West Indies, the rest in February 1796. Landed at Barbados, took part in capture of St.Lucia from late April, earning Gen.Abercromby's praise. 1st Bn to Grenada, June 1796, and saw much action; transferred in August to Martinique, where joined by 2nd Bn in November. Over 1,000 strong on arrival in the islands, disease reduced the unit to below 650 by November. On 15.2.1797, 30 officers and 343 men took part in capture of Trinidad from Spanish; but were part of British forces repulsed by Spanish at San Juan, Puerto Rico, 17–30.4.1797. On Martinique from June, mustering 623 all ranks including 50 gunners. Disbanded at St.Pierre, Martinique, 25.12.1797; men sent to Barbados to form, with drafts from other units, new 5th Rifle Battalion, 60th Foot. *Uniform:* See illustration and Plates B and F.

Loewenstein's Fusiliers Prince Loewenstein also raised in Germany, from 22.8.1795, a light infantry corps with eight companies each of four officers and 137 men; two companies were armed with rifles. Sent to Isle of Wight in July 1796, to the West Indies in December. On Martinique until it took part in unsuccessful siege of San Juan, Puerto Rico, April 1797. Many deserters, these often reported by Spanish as being 'French'—which may indicate that unit might have drafted French POWs. To Barbados still 800 strong; incorporated into 5th (Rifle) Bn, 60th Foot, 18.12.1797.

Uniform: Black round hat, black cockade, green plume; red coatee with green collar, cuffs, lapels and turnbacks, brass buttons; white breeches, black gaiters; white accoutrements for fusiliers, black for rifle companies.

Loewenstein's Light Infantry Regiment The third unit raised in Bavaria from June 1800 by Prince Loewenstein, to have about 1,000 men divided into nine companies. Deployed in Nuremberg area, where it fought French in November and December. Following Peace of Lunéville, sent to Trieste and embarked for Malta, May 1801. July 1801, part of reinforcements sent to Egypt; engaged 23 August near Cairo; back to Malta in November. On Isle of Wight, April 1802, where disbanded 14 May still 450 strong; incorporated into 5th Rifle Battalion, 60th Foot.

Uniform: Black round hat, black cockade and plume; blue-grey coatee with green collar, cuffs, lapels and turnbacks, brass buttons; blue-grey breeches, black half-gaiters; black accoutrements; rifles with sword-bayonets.

Loyal Emigrant Raised from 25.5.1793 by Claude-Louis, Comte de Châtres-Nançay, with establishment of 721 men in ten-company battalion, with half-company of gunners serving two 6pdr. guns. Formed in London area from French émigrés; sent to Flanders at end of May; two companies of chasseurs added at Ostend. From 16 August, engaged against French Republican forces in Dunkirk area until withdrawn

The Maltese Artificers raised in 1801 for the expedition to Egypt had the same uniform as the Royal Military Artificers. From 1797 to 1802 dress uniform consisted of a blue coat with black collar, cuffs and shoulder straps, yellow lace, brass buttons and white turnbacks; white breeches, black gaiters, and a bicorn with white plume. At left, a sergeant with pike, crimson sash with black central line; centre, a corporal with yellow shoulder strap and wing; right, back view of a private. (Print after Connolly)

towards Bruges in September, having already gained excellent fighting reputation. Engaged during autumn along Ostend Canal; independent German company attached, 25.10.1793; veteran company formed, 1.11.1793, by which date regiment had two battalions and was at Bruges. In Menin area early 1794; heavily engaged May/June, retreated with Duke of York's remaining forces following fall of Ypres, 18 June. Large detachment lost at surrender of Nieuport, 19 July; the two chasseur companies and German company wiped out and some 200 émigré prisoners executed by French. Engaged in several actions as Allies withdrew into Hanover; from over 1,260 all ranks in May, strength down to 450 by November 1794.

Evacuated to England, May 1795, but landed at Carnac, Brittany, with Hervilly's Regiment on 27 June; volunteer Compagnie Bretonne raised locally and detached to serve with *chouans* in the interior. Regiment engaged in the series of disastrous actions at Quiberon until 21 July

Working dress of the Royal Military Artificers from 1795, doubtless worn by the Maltese Artificers. Black round hat; blue jacket with black collar and cuffs, brass buttons, yellow lace at the collar; white waistcoat and gaiter-trousers. Private at left, sergeant at right with a red hat tuft, gold lace hat band and on collar. (Print after Connolly)

when survivors – 12 officers and 85 men – embarked for England. Compagnie Bretonne continued guerrilla warfare, instructing Royalist partisans and ambushing Republican troops as late as November 1799. Regiment reorganised during autumn 1795 with new recruits and, on 8 October, drafted in remnants of Béon, Damas, Périgord, Rohan and Salm (qqv); up to about 350 men by late December. At Lymington during 1796; veteran company re-raised, company of gentlemen volunteers added in December, but still only about 360 all ranks.

January 1797, embarked at Falmouth for Portugal, landing 6 February. Discipline poor; June 1797, gentlemen volunteer company disbanded for insubordination, some officers relieved of duty by Gen.Stuart. Regiment later reported up to establishment, in excellent order and fit for service. Deployed at Abrantes in 1801 to cover retreat of Portuguese from invading Spanish during 'War of the Oranges' but did not see action. Shipped to Jersey following Peace of Amiens, and disbanded 24.8.1802.

Uniform: 1793–97 See illustration and Plate D. Chasseur companies had coatees and light infantry caps. German independent company had, in 1793, besides the red coat faced yellow, a sky blue frock with red collar and cuffs, a 'German style' hat with red plume and black cockade. *From 1797* See Plate H.

Lüninck Light infantry regiment raised in Dutch service from August 1794 by Paul-François-Bernard, Baron de Lüninck; followed British retreat into Hanover. Passed into British pay April 1795 at Wohlbrücken, but disbanded in May.

Uniform: Green coat with green collar, lapels and cuffs, red turnbacks, white buttonhole lace, pewter buttons; red waistcoat; green breeches with white lace, black half-gaiters; round hat with brim turned up both sides, bearskin crest, green turban with thin white metal chain, green cockade and plume; black accoutrements. Silver buttons and lace for officers.

Maltese Artillery Company (also called Franco-Maltese Artillery Company). Recruited among Maltese in Corsica for British service in spring 1795; Chevalier de Sade, French émigré naval officer, commissioned captain on 5 May; strength of four officers and 70 gunners. Evacuated to Elba, October 1796; and to Portugal, landing Lisbon 21.6.1797. Amalgamated 26 June with Royal French Marine Artillery Company (qv), which in turn incorporated into Rotalier's émigré artillery regiment (qv), 1.1.1798. *Uniform:* See Plate H.

Maltese Chasseurs (also called Maltese Light Infantry). In spring 1800 British forces overran most of Malta, and French retreated into Valetta fortifications. The British began raising 'Maltese Independent Companies', four being formed by May with another four recruiting. By June, led by Thomas Graham, corps up to eight 100-strong companies and named Maltese Chasseurs or 'Cacciatori Maltese'. Took part in siege of Valetta until French surrender on 8 September. Three companies participated in defence of Elba, 1801. Disbanded in 1802.

Uniform: Rankers had single-breasted, hip-length, light blue-grey jacket without turnbacks, with red collar, cuffs, shoulder straps, red cloth covered wood buttons, wide red Maltese-style sash around waist tying at back; buckskin gaiter-trousers; nankeen jacket and gaiter-trousers in summer; round hat with green plume at left; black accoutrements;

Périgord Regiment, 1794–95. Red coatee, black collar, cuffs, lapels, turnbacks and shoulder straps, yellow piping, brass buttons stamped with a fleur-de-lis; white waistcoat and breeches, black gaiters; black cap with transverse foxtail crest, brass bugle horn badge, black and yellow cockade. Officers wore gold buttons and lace. (Anne S.K.Brown Military Collection, Brown University, Providence. Photo R.Chartrand)

French muskets, bayonets and hangers.

Maltese Coast Artillery Two companies raised from 1800 (see Vol.2).

Maltese Pioneers, Maltese Artificers Pioneer battalion of 540 men raised on Malta, at Gen.Abercromby's request; with his army in Egypt during 1801 but does not appear to have seen action. Corps of Maltese Artificers, also raised for Egyptian expedition, was probably part of, or even the same unit as the Maltese Pioneers. *Uniform:* Artificers had same uniform as British Royal Military Artificers, which may have also been worn by Pioneers. See illustrations.

Maltese Provincial Battalions Two battalions raised from 1802 for garrison service in Malta (see Vol.2).

Maréchaussée & Guides (Haiti) A constabulary cavalry corps was in place when the British occupied part of Saint-Domingue (Haiti) in 1793; its value was clearly appreciated, as some 300 troopers (50 white, 100 mulatto and 50 black) were reported in British pay in 1794 (PRO, WO 6/5). Reorganised 26.12.1795 into 44 'brigades' totalling 430 all ranks (PRO, T81/14). Often reported fighting in skirmishes; some 250 on duty May 1797 despite loss of Mirebalais district. Probably dissolved when British evacuated Haiti in 1798.

Uniform: The same as during French Royal regime: blue coat with red collar, cuffs, lapels and turnbacks, pewter buttons; white waistcoat and breeches; hat edged white with white cockade; buff accoutrements edged white, blue bandoleer edged white with silver fleur-de-lis edged scarlet, blue housings edged white.

Mauger Regiment of 1,252 men authorised raised in Germany 12.5.1795 by Comte de Mauger for service in West Indies. Only a few men enlisted and the corps was never formed.

Meuron Swiss regiment raised 1781 for Dutch colonial service. Arrived at Cape of Good Hope in January 1783; campaigned with the French; and stationed in Ceylon (Sri Lanka), then a Dutch colony, from 1786. In 1795 British forces landed in Ceylon; six companies of regiment were captured at Trincomalee at end of August after losing 42 men in unequal combat; Governor of Ceylon at Colombo surrendered to British 5.2.1796. In Europe meanwhile, Col.Comte de Meuron – unpaid by Dutch for eight months – signed agreement 30.3.1795 transferring regiment to British service; transfer actually took place in Ceylon on 14 October. It was to have ten companies, including grenadiers and chasseurs, with total of 1,287 officers and men. Companies were posted in Ceylon and southern India, later assembled for Mysore campaign against Tipoo Sahib in late 1798; took part in battle of Malavelly (27.2.1799), and noted for bravery in assault and capture of Seringapatam (4.5.1799). Remained stationed at Vellore and Madras, India, into early 1800s. (See also Vol.2)

Uniform: In Dutch service, blue coat with yellow collar, cuffs and turnbacks, white square-ended lace loops, pewter buttons; white waistcoat and breeches; black leather dragoon-style helmet with brass plate and trim, black horsehair mane, white plume. For dress in British service, see illustration.

Minorca Light Dragoons Company of three officers and 58 troopers raised in 1800 from Hungarians in Minorca Regiment (qv). Remained at Minorca, and disbanded about 1802.

Minorca Regiment (or Stuart's Minorca Regiment). Following British capture of Minorca, 1798, they found among Spanish prisoners of war over 1,000 'Germans' of a Swiss regiment; these had been previously captured by French from Austrians, and 'sold' to the Spanish for two dollars a head.... Enlisted by Sir Charles Stuart into British service and formed as Minorca Regiment from 25.12.1798. To Gibraltar, October 1800, and to Egypt in January 1801; regiment distinguished at battle of Alexandria, 21 March, repulsing French cavalry and capturing an infantry colour, at cost of 300 casualties out of about 975. Stuart's remained in Egypt until 1802, when styled 'Queen's Own Germans' in recognition of excellent service. (See also Vol.2)

Uniform: See MAA 79, *Napoleon's Egyptian Campaigns 1798–1801*, p.30, for interesting portrait of Private Anton Lütz, c.1802, shown holding colour of 3rd Bn, 21st Half-Brigade which he captured at Alexandria on 21.3.1801. Being illiterate he could not be promoted to sergeant, so was rewarded with cash and a left breast badge showing the captured colour. The red coatee had a yellow collar and cuffs, square white evenly-set loops (later with a black line) and pewter buttons; it was worn with a white waistcoat and breeches, and a black bicorn with a short white-over-red plume. This was replaced by the stovepipe shako from c.1801. Officers had silver buttons and lace.

Moluccas Volunteer Corps Formed at Madras with 500 volunteers from several Indian native infantry battalions who signed for three-year enlistments following capture of Dutch island of Ternate in the Moluccas on 21.6.1801. Left for Ternate in October 1801, serving there until island evacuated by British in September 1803.

Montalembert's Chasseurs Britanniques de Saint-Domingue See MAA 294 *British Forces in the West Indies 1793–1815.*

Montmorency-Laval French émigré 'white cockade' infantry regiment raised in Holland from 1.8.1794; only 150 strong by June 1795. Disbanded in Hanover 24.10.1795, most joining Condé's Army. *Uniform:* Red coatee, yellow collar, cuffs, turnbacks and shoulder straps, white piping, pewter buttons stamped '6'; white waistcoat and breeches, black gaiters; black round hat with bearskin crest and red turban, white cockade, loop and plume.

Mortemart French émigré 'white cockade' infantry regiment raised in Holland from 1.8.1794; about 160 all ranks by September. Retreated into Hanover, January 1795, then numbering 257; recruited up to over 400 by June so was not disbanded; went to Stade and embarked for England in November. From 1.1.1796 reorganised as one-battalion regiment of ten companies with additional Noble Chasseurs company; sent to Guernsey in February, spent 1796 in Channel Islands. To Portugal, January 1797; reportedly 700 strong when stationed at Lisbon. June 1801, deployed in Abrantes area to cover Portuguese retreat but saw no action beyond a few skirmishes with Spanish. July 1801, Noble Chasseurs company sent back to England to be incorporated into Foreign Veterans (qv). Mortemart's stayed in Lisbon until early August 1802, when embarked for England; disbanded Portsmouth, 24.8.1802.

Uniform: 1794 Red coatee, black collar, cuffs, turnbacks and shoulder straps, white piping, pewter buttons stamped '7'; white waistcoat and breeches, black gaiters; black round hat with bearskin crest and red turban, white cockade, loop and plume. *1798* See Plate H.

Pionniers du Quartier Général (Pioneers of the Headquarters), c.1794. Red coatee, blue collar, cuffs, shoulder straps, turnbacks and pantaloons, pewter buttons; round hat with white band, loop and plume, black cockade. (Anne S.K.Brown Military Collection, Brown University, Providence. Photo R.Chartrand)

Rohan's 1st Hussar Regiment, 1794–96. Sky blue dolman with scarlet collar and cuffs; white pelisse with black fur trim, brass buttons, yellow cords; sky blue breeches trimmed yellow, crimson and yellow sash, black boots edged yellow; black shako with white plume and yellow cords; sky blue sabretache trimmed yellow, sky blue housings edged yellow, white sheepskin. (Anne S.K.Brown Military Collection, Brown University, Providence. Photo R.Chartrand)

Périgord Émigré light infantry regiment authorised raised in Germany from 10.7.1794 under command of Comte du Périgord; only one company recruited by December. Evacuated to England June 1795, landing at Quiberon on 17 July 150 strong; annihilated in next nine days of fighting, only 16 men being listed among survivors. *Uniform:* See illustration.

Pfaffenhofen Legion of Germans raised in Dutch service from 27.12.1794 by François-Simon, Comte Pfaff de Pfaffenhoffen, to consist of infantry, hussars and artillery. Passed into British pay 5.5.1795 in Hanover, to have 1,200 infantry and 800 hussars. Hundreds were enlisted but deserted just as quickly and, after various disputes, British government forbade further enlistment on 24 August and transferred remnants into Rohan's Hussars (qv).

Pioneers of the Headquarters (also called French Corps of Pioneers). Émigré company raised in Low Countries late in 1794 under Capt.de Selliard and attached to Duke of York's staff; disbanded 16.1.1796. *Uniform:* See illustration.

Power's Chasseurs Two companies of chasseurs raised in Belgium from 9.9.1794 by Capt.Harris Power, 37th Foot, to have ten officers and 214 men. About 100 were actually enlisted, and followed British retreat into Hanover in early 1795. Probably incorporated into Hardy's Royal York Fusiliers (qv), May 1795. *Uniform:* Green coatee, black collar, cuffs and turnbacks, pewter buttons; grey pantaloons, black half-gaiters; round hat or cap, black forage cap; black accoutrements; armed with rifles and short swords.

HOLLAND & GERMANY, 1794-95:
1: Fusilier, Vioménil's Regiment
2: Officer, Autichamp's Regiment
3: Grenadier, Broglie's Regiment
4: Gunner, Rotalier's Artillery

A

HOLLAND & GERMANY, 1794-95:
1: Officer, Waldstein's Light Infantry
2: Rifleman, York Rangers (Ramsay's)
3: Rifleman, Hompesch's Chasseurs
4: Rifleman, Lowenstein's Chasseurs

P. Courcelle

B

HOLLAND & GERMANY, 1794-95:
1: Hussar, Damas' Legion
2: Hussar, 2nd Regt., Rohan Hussars
3: Gunner, Salm-Kirburg Horse Artillery

C

QUIBERON, 1795:
1: Fusilier, Hector's Royal Marine
2: Officer, Salm-Kirburg Light Infantry
3: Fusilier, Breton Co., Loyal Emigrant Regt.
4: Duc de Choiseul

P. Courcelle

D

HAITI, 1795-98:
1: Officer, Uhlans Britanniques, 1796
2: Fusilier, Gendarmes Royaux Anglais, 1795
3: Trooper, York Hussars, 1796-98

P. Courcelle

E

EASTERN CARIBBEAN, 1796-97
1: Rifleman, Royal York Fusiliers
2: Fusilier, Royal-Étranger Regiment
3: Rifleman, Lowentstein's Chasseurs

1

3

2

P. Courcelle

F

MALTA & EGYPT, 1799-1802:
1: Fusilier, Corsican Rangers; Egypt, 1801
2: Fusilier, Watteville's Regt.; Malta & Egypt, 1801-02
3: Officer, Roll's Regiment; Egypt, 1801
4: Trooper, Hompesch's Mounted Rifles

PORTUGAL, 1797-1802:
1: Sergeant, Maltese Artillery Co., 1797-98
2: Grenadier, Castries' Regiment, 1797-99
3: Fusilier, Loyal Emigrant Regiment, 1797-99
4: Fusilier, Mortemart's Regiment, 1801-02

P. Courcelle

1

2

3

4

H

Rohan's Hussars Two hussar regiments raised by Louis-Victor, Prince de Rohan in Germany: 1st, from 3.3.1794, with establishment of eight companies each of three officers and 109 men, was recruited up to strength. Soon distinguished itself in action with British expeditionary force against French in Holland. Retreated to Germany with British forces, January 1795. 2nd Regiment raised from 12.6.1795, had about 300 all ranks by late September when embarked for England. 1st Rohan's Hussars, some 920 strong, were awaiting embarkation in Germany when news came that they were to be sent to West Indies; two companies mutinied, refused to embark and deserted, cutting their way out with their sabres. Both regiments amalgamated from 26.11.1795 to form ten-company regiment of 55 officers and 1,119 men. Shipped to England and on to Haiti in early 1796. Over 1,000 strong in May 1796; distinguished itself in attack on Bombarde, June; but ravages of fever reduced unit to 600 by October and, despite drafts of reinforcements, only 39 officers and 340 men survived by June 1797. Regiment apparently disbanded 1.7.1797, remnants passing into York Hussars (qv). *Uniform: 1st Regiment* See illustration; *2nd Regiment* See Plate C.

Rohan's Light Infantry Raised by Prince de Rohan from 3.3.1794 with establishment of six companies, each of four officers and 138 men. By July it had 741 all ranks including 36 gunners for battalion guns. In action against French in Holland, distinguished itself at Appelthorn on 19 October. Saw more action during retreat into Germany in February 1795, losing its guns; embarked for England, and thence to Quiberon, landing on 17 July. Fought gallantly but, of 300 men who landed only 84 returned to Isle d'Yeu. Others had remained in England, but corps disbanded 8.10.1795, survivors passing into Loyal Emigrant (qv). *Uniform:* See illustration.

Roll Regiment raised in Switzerland for British service from 9.12.1794 by Baron Louis de Roll, former officer in French Swiss Guards, to have two battalions of ten companies each including flank companies, with establishment of 1,698 men – recruits mainly from Switzerland, Alsace and Germany. Sent to Corsica, April-October 1796, thence to Elba. Two companies took part in raid on Tuscan coast, November 1796. When Elba evacuated, April 1797, de Roll's was transferred to Portugal; reduced to one battalion, November 1798. Moved to Minorca, September 1799; to Gibraltar, October 1800; joined Abercromby's army in Egypt where it distinguished itself in action during March 1801 at Alexandria. Remained in Egypt until June 1803 when transferred to Gibraltar. (See also Vol.2)

Uniform: Red coatee, royal blue collar, cuffs and turnbacks, six white loops in front and two to each side of collar, white piping, pewter buttons; white waistcoat and breeches, black half-gaiters; round hat with fur crest, red turban, white-over-red plume; plain fur cap with white cords and plume for grenadiers. *In Portugal* the corps had red coat, royal blue collar, cuffs and lapels piped white, white lace at buttonholes and collar, white turnbacks, pewter buttons; white waistcoat and breeches; probably a bicorn hat. *From 1801* red coatee, sky blue collar and cuffs, white buttonhole loops, pewter buttons; white breeches; stovepipe shako. *In Egypt* men were sketched wearing plain round hats and white gaiter-trousers. See Plate G for officers.

Rohan's Light Infantry, 1794–95. Red coatee, sky blue collar, cuffs, half-lapels with five buttons and turnbacks piped white, pewter buttons; white waistcoat and breeches, black gaiters; black felt cylindrical cap with, at top left, black cockade (changed to white at Quiberon), white loop and plume, in front a black felt plate edged yellow with central yellow star. Officers had silver buttons and epaulettes. (Anne S.K.Brown Military Collection, Brown University, Providence. Photo R.Chartrand)

Rovéréa's Swiss Regiment, 1799–1800; officer (left) and enlisted men. The first uniform was a green coatee with black collar and cuffs, green turnbacks edged with wide black lace, and brass buttons; green waistcoat, sky blue Hungarian-style long breeches, black half-gaiters; and a black shako with black turban edged yellow, black cockade with yellow loop, black plume for fusiliers, white for grenadiers and green for chasseurs; white accoutrements were issued. From c.1800 the uniform was much the same but the turnbacks were black, the waistcoat had two rows of brass buttons, the shako had no cockade but a yellow-tipped black plume for fusiliers. Rovéréa's appears to have been the only Swiss unit in British service which wore the red armband and did not wear the Austrian insignia of a green oakleaf on the shako. Officers had coats and bicorns. (Print after Martinet)

Rotalier's French Emigrant Artillery Raised from 1.11.1794, to consist of two half-battalions each of four companies; each company was to have 116 officers and men, two 8pdr. and six 4pdr. (captured French) guns with limbers and ammunition wagons, and 70 horses. One half-battalion was to be raised by Count Pierre-Alexis de Rotalier, former field officer in French Royal Corps of Artillery, the other by M.de Quiefdeville – who was unable to recruit his half battalion and was dismissed in May 1795. Rotalier's companies up to establishment by January 1795, and by June up to 600 all ranks. In southern England until embarked with 10 guns and landed at Carnac, Brittany, on 27.6.1795, forming artillery park at Portivy. Took part in capture of Fort Penthièvre, 3 July; engagements on 6th, 7th and 16th. Part of regiment was at Quiberon when it fell on 21 July, but many were at Portivy and about 440 officers and men were evacuated to England. October 1796, reduced to three companies each of 78 men; embarked for Portugal, November; 26.1.1797, Franco-Maltese Artillery Company (qv) attached to Rotalier's. Stationed at Feitoria and, from 1801, Berquinha, Belem and Lisbon; proposed permanent transfer to Portuguese service came to nothing. Returned to England, and disbanded at Gosport 24.8.1802. *Uniform:* See Plate A.

Rovéréa Swiss regiment of 14 companies, including two of chasseurs, raised spring 1799 and commanded by Col.Ferdinand-Isaac de Rovéréa, formerly of Erlacht's Swiss in French Royal service. Joined Austro-Swiss forces and saw action at Murg, 19.5.1799, and many skirmishes. At Kempten a new agreement stipulated a two- battalion regiment of 2,025 men in December, field command passing to Col.Watteville. In action 1800 against French invaders of Switzerland; chasseurs almost wiped out at Rechberg, and regiment badly mauled at Moeskirch, 1.5 and 5.5.1800.

Royal Étranger Regiment buttons, c.1796–97, found on Grenada, West Indies. Above, brass button with crowned RE and motto TOUJOURS FIDELES AU ROI ('Always faithful to the King'). Below, brass button with RL for Royal Liègois, later renamed Royal Étranger. The uniform was a medium or sky blue coat with red collar, black lapels and cuffs edged with white piping, white turnbacks, yellow loops; white waistcoat, sky blue breeches; fur caps with white plume and cords. Officers had bicorns with a silver cockade loop and white plume, gold buttons, lace and epaulettes. (Mr.& Mrs.Don Troiani Collection)

Royal York Fusiliers (Hardy's), 1794–96. Black cap with transverse foxtail; green coatee with red-piped black collar, shoulder straps and cuffs (cut indented in 'V'-shape, with one button), red piping in front and edging the green turnbacks, and brass buttons. Red waistcoat with black and yellow cords and piping, green pantaloons with red piping, black half-gaiters edged red. Armed with muskets, some with rifles; brass-hilted hangers, black accoutrements. Later changes included adding a green feather and bugle horn to the cap, red shoulder straps and turnbacks, and white accoutrements. Officers had gilt buttons and gold piping instead of red, and often had a bicorn with green tipped red plume. (Anne S.K.Brown Military Collection, Brown University, Providence. Photo R.Chartrand)

Armistice signed 16.7.1800; regiment sent from Ingolstadt to Amberg and into Bohemia in winter 1800–1801. Swiss corps in British service were assembled at Marburg in February 1801 and disbanded from 20 May. Some 30 officers and 200 men of Rovéréa joined Watteville's new regiment (qv) three days later. *Uniform:* See illustration.

Royal Anglo-Corsican Battalions Three battalions raised in Corsica from November 1794, each of ten companies and staff totalling 568 Corsican officers and men; fourth raised from June 1795; reduced to two, late 1795. Deployed against bandits; part of 2nd Bn took part in capture of Elba, July 1796. Tensions increased between Corsican and British soldiers as time passed, as did desertions; when British evacuated Corsica in October 1796 the battalions refused to embark, and dissolved. *Uniform:* Red coat with white-piped blue collar, cuffs and lapels, white turnbacks, pewter buttons; red waistcoat, tight blue long trousers, black half-gaiters; black bicorn with white cockade loop, black cockade and white plume; brown hooded greatcoat.

Royal-Étranger 'Royal Foreigners' regiment raised in Germany from 7.5.1795 by Comte de la Tour (also called Royal-Liégeois until late 1795). Establishment of eight companies each of 150 men plus a 50-strong

artillery company; many Dutch recruits, the remainder being Germans, with mostly French émigré officers. To England, January 1796, and thence to West Indies in February. May/June, campaigned against Fédon's 'brigands' on St.Lucia; fought on Grenada from late June; detachment also sent to help quell the Caribs on St.Vincent. Yellow fever reduced the regiment from 1,035 men in June 1796 to 707 in January 1797. New recruits brought the strength up to 1,300 including 50 gunners; nevertheless, ordered disbanded and incorporated on Grenada and Barbados into 3rd Bn, 60th Foot on 1.1.1798, and into the Foreign Artillery on 18.4.1798. Sir John Moore praised the regiment when on St.Lucia, but his superior Sir Ralph Abercromby, Commander-in-Chief West Indies, felt it lacked discipline. *Uniform:* See illustration of buttons, and Plate F.

Royal Foreign Artillery See MAA 294 *British Forces in the West Indies 1793–1815.*

Royal French Marine Artillery Independent Company During occupation of Toulon by an Anglo-Spanish force, Royalist gunners of French naval and army artillery helped them defend the city. Evacuated to Elba by the British on 18.12.1793, they formed independent artillery company of 70 men in January 1794. Went to Corsica in July; returned to Elba in October 1796; thence to Portugal, landing Lisbon 21.6.1797. Shortly thereafter, amalgamated with Maltese Artillery Company (qv). *Uniform:* Initially that of the French Marine Artillery (see MAA 227 *Napoleon's Sea Soldiers*). Complete clothing was issued in Corsica including the full uniform and a fatigue dress consisting on a round hat, flannel waistcoat and breeches, linen pantaloons, blue stockings.

Royal Louis Regiment raised 'in the name and for the service of Louis XVII' in British pay from 7.9.1793 at Toulon, then occupied by the

Soldiers of Swiss regiments in British service, 1799–1801. All wear green jackets with various facings, sky blue trousers and shakos (see text for description of regiments).

RIGHT **Salm-Kirburg Light Infantry, 1794–95.** Red coatee with red collar, black cuffs and turnbacks, white lace at sleeve buttonholes, pewter buttons; white waistcoat, grey breeches, black half-gaiters; round hat with brim turned up on left, black bearskin crest, red turban, black plume;, white accoutrements. (Anne S.K.Brown Military Collection, Brown University, Providence. Photo R.Chartrand)

Salm-Kirburg Hussars, 1794–95. Scarlet dolman with black collar and cuffs, white cords; black pelisse with scarlet cords, white fur, pewter buttons; white and black sash, black breeches trimmed with scarlet cords, black boots edged scarlet; black mirleton cap with white wing, cords and plume; red sabretache edged black with crowned 'GR' in black and white cord; white sheepskin edged red, scarlet valise edged white. Armed with sabre and carbine; black accoutrements. (Anne S.K.Brown Military Collection, Brown University, Providence. Photo R.Chartrand)

British, Spanish and Piedmontese. Officers commissioned by Prince Regent of France; regiment used French drills and discipline, and was to consist of six companies each of 120 men including grenadiers. By 12.10.1793 unit had recruited 395 all ranks and had already seen action in a counter-attack against the besieging Republicans on 1 October. Lost several officers and 40 men resisting, with part of 30th Foot, a heavy French attack which eventually captured an outwork. Another 30 were lost in an abortive sortie on 29–30 October; and on 14 December some 77 men out of 300 were killed or wounded defending Fort Mulgrave. Royal Louis gained British esteem for its excellent conduct; it was the last unit evacuated from Toulon by Adm.Hood's fleet, leaving behind over 100 men including 80 wounded covering the last evacuees. Royal Louis was reformed on Elba. May-August 1794, part of regiment took part in capture of Corsica. Meanwhile in London, Secretary of State Henry Dundas felt Royal Louis should be incorporated into new émigré regiments forming in England; Gen.Sir Gilbert Elliot tried vainly to countermand the decision but, in November, the regiment arrived at Portsmouth about 475 strong, and was incorporated into Hervilly's Regiment (qv) on 12.12.1794.

Uniform: White coat, blue collar, cuffs and lapels, white turnbacks with blue fleur-de-lis, white shoulder straps edged blue, brass buttons stamped with three fleurs-de-lis and '1'; white waistcoat and breeches; black bicorn with white cockade and cockade loop. French M1777 musket, white accoutrements. *Grenadiers* had bearskin cap with brass

37

plate stamped with fleur-de-lis, white cords and red plume; red fringed epaulettes, red flaming grenade turnback ornaments. *Drummers* wore French Royal livery: blue coat with red facings, white chain on crimson livery lace. The uniform was of French Royal army style, cut according to 1791 regulations; NCO's had French rank distinctions. Officers had gold buttons and epaulettes.

Royal York Fusiliers (also called Hardy's Royal York Fusiliers). Raised from Germans by Maj.Thomas C.Hardy from 26.9.1794, to have ten companies each of four officers and 112 men, plus artillery detachment. All officers to be British except 15 subalterns from the gentry of Flanders. Served with Duke of York's army in Flanders from autumn 1794; retreated into Hanover, January 1795; embarked for England in September; thence to West Indies, late February 1796, with 33 officers and 672 men. Took part in capture of St.Lucia, 3.-24.5.1796, where it remained in garrison. Reduced by disease to 130 men by May 1797, Col.Hardy being amongst the dead. Remnants incorporated into 3rd Bn, 60th Foot on 20 May although formally disbanded only on 25 August. *Uniform:* See illustration and Plate F.

Saint Helena Corps of Lascars The South Atlantic island of St.Helena was under Honourable East India Company administration, and garrisoned by its own establishment of troops recruited in Britain and locally. In July 1795 it was proposed to form an artillery unit from Malays left on the island from captured Dutch ships; Asians in naval and artillery service were usually called Lascars. Two companies were formed, probably during August, and were reported excellent at gunnery practice in September. Disbandment date unknown.

Uniform: July proposal specified a coarse cloth jacket, two pairs of long drawers, two shirts, a hat and presumably shoes.

Salis Raised from 14.7.1799 in Switzerland by Baron Rodolphe de Salis-Marschlins, former general in the French Royal army, to have six fusilier companies and one of chasseurs. In action June 1800 at Kempten; defence of Feldkirch, 13 July; thereafter retreated into Tyrol. Fought at Zutz, Casanova and Zernetz in December 1799; sent to Mahrburg in Styria following armistice of January 1801, and disbanded 15.3.1801. On 23 May five officers and 200 men joined Watteville's new regiment (qv). *Uniform:* Green coatee, sky blue collar, cuffs and turnbacks, brass buttons; sky blue pantaloons, black half-gaiters; black shako with black turban, yellow cockade loop, black cockade, yellow plume tipped black, green oakleaf; white accoutrements. Chasseurs had the same as fusiliers except for their pantherskin turban, yellow loop on left side (but no cockade), and green plume, and carried rifles.

Salm-Kirburg Hussars German unit, raised from December 1791 by Prince Maurice of Salm-Kirburg. After campaigning 1792–93 with Prince of Condé the regiment was taken into British service from 22.2.1794. The Prince of Salm-Kirburg agreed to provide regiment of hussars, now to consist of eight companies with company of horse artillery and totalling of 912 men, and to raise regiment of light infantry (see below); 450 hussars and artillerymen joined Duke of York's army in August, retreating into Hanover in January 1795. Regiment refused to leave Germany; disbanded at Wildeshausen, 3.12.1795. *Uniform: Hussars*

See illustration. *Artillery:* See Plate C.

Warren Hussars, officer, 1795. Red dolman with blue collar, cuffs, cords and breeches; sky blue pelisse with black fur, silver cords and buttons for officers. Sketch by Cecil C.P.Lawson after the portrait of the Comte de Contades, colonel of the unit. According to C.H.Smith, troopers had a red dolman with blue collar and cuffs, blue cords, sky blue breeches, black cylindrical cap with white plume, and red sabretache with white edge, crown and 'GR'. (Journal of the Society for Army Historical Research, 1943)

Salm-Kirburg Light Infantry German unit raised by Prince of Salm-Kirburg from 22.2.1794, to have six companies totalling 850 men. Joined British forces in Holland, October 1794; in action December along Waal river; distinguished itself with a detachment of Foot Guards at Arnhem in January. More fighting in February, but regiment had by now lost a third of strength; 22.6.1795, 150 survivors embarked on British ships. Took part in disastrous Quiberon expedition, July; only 18 men escaped, and passed into Loyal Emigrant (qv) on 8.8.1795. *Uniform:* See illustration and Plate D.

Prince Maurice of Salm-Kirburg meanwhile tried to raise another German infantry regiment of 1,300 men in British pay from 8.6.1795, but with little response. Less that 400 eventually reached the Isle of Wight, and were also drafted into Loyal Emigrant on 13 December.

Uhlans (or Hulans) Britanniques Mounted corps of two squadrons, each of two companies, raised in Belgium from 2.11.1793 by Louis, Comte de Bouillé; mostly ex-soldiers of French Royal army with some Swiss and Germans. Attached to British army in Flanders from November 1793, saw action in many skirmishes. Initially with 250 men, raised to 350 in February 1794 at Menin; third squadron added in June, but only 300 present out of establishment of 600 by September. Fought with distinction at Gerdermalsen, 9.1.1795, one squadron making brilliant charge over ice and snow. During retreat into Hanover noted both for keeping French patrols at bay but also for its plundering. In August 1795, 361 all ranks evacuated to England and immediately sent to Quiberon, but were not landed. On 18.3.1796 some 450 men sailed for West Indies, landing at St.Lucia and serving on foot there during May/June. Returned to England, and disbanded at Spithead on 18 August. However, four companies were sent to Haiti, arriving in October, to be incorporated into Montalembert's (qv) Légion britannique de Saint-Domingue. *Uniform:* See illustration and Plate E.

Uhlans (or Hulans) Britanniques de Saint-Domingue (Charmilly's) See MAA 294 *British Forces in the West Indies 1793–1815.*

Villettes Commission granted to Col.Villettes, 4.4.1799, to raise regiment of Albanians (unit sometimes called Albion, possibly corruption of 'Albanian'). Villettes and a few officers went to Corfu to recruit, but nothing came of it. *Uniform:* Red coatee, yellow collar and cuffs, white loops, pewter buttons; white breeches (C.Hamilton Smith MS).

Vioménil 'White cockade' regiment raised by Comte Charles du Houx de Vioménil (or Viomesni) from 1.8.1794. Could only muster 266 men in June 1795 when based at Dillenburg, Nassau; disbanded near Rottenburg, Swabia, 25.10.1795. *Uniform:* See Plate A.

Waldstein Light infantry unit raised by Comte Ferdinand-Ernest de Waldstein in Waldeck, Germany, from 12.7.1795, to have eight companies of five officers and 150 men each. Went to England, August 1796; posted on Isle of Wight. Left for West Indies 23.4.1797 over 800 strong; to Martinique with detachment on Dominica. By 1.4.1798, having seen no action, Waldstein's had been reduced by fever to 500 men, who were drafted into 4th Bn, 60th Foot that month. *Uniform: 1795* See Plate B. *West Indies* Green coatee, sky blue collar, cuffs, half-lapels and turnbacks,

brass buttons; sky blue trousers with yellow stripe, black half-gaiters; round hat with black plume at left; black accoutrements. Hamilton Smith shows his figure armed with a rifle.

Warren's Hussars Unit of about 60 troopers raised in 1795 to provide cavalry support for Quiberon expedition, and named in honour of Adm.Warren who commanded the Royal Navy squadron. Only nine survived Quiberon, and served on nearby Ile d'Yeu until December 1795; disbanded 24.1.1796 after return to England. *Uniform:* See illustration.

Watteville Swiss regiment formed by Frédéric Baron de Watteville from 1.5.1801, following peace treaty of Lunéville signed that February. Officers and men from Rovéréa's, Courten's, Bachmann's and Salis' (qqv) disbanded Swiss regiments in British pay, and three officers and 92 men from Durand's of the Prince of Condé's disbanded army. Ten companies, including grenadiers and chasseurs, totalling 42 officers and 1,053 rank and file. Quickly moved to Trieste; embarked on British ships in June, arriving on Malta on 8 July. In August, light company and one fusilier company took part in operations leading to British evacuation of Elba. Remainder sailed from Malta 22 July and landed in Egypt early August. Col.de Watteville later noted that 'A Sphinx and a crown of laurels with the word EGYPT were embroidered on the colours (in 1804), on account of the conduct of the Regiment, during the blockade of Alexandria.' Back in Malta by October, Watteville's was sent back to Egypt again in late 1801 and remained in garrison until 1803. (See Vol.2) *Uniform:* See Plate G.

Wittgenstein Infantry regiment raised in Dutch pay from July 1794 by Chrétien-Louis-Casimir, Comte Sayn-Wittgenstein, to have 900 men. Retreated into Hanover, January 1795; passed into British service, 28.2.1796, to have four companies each of three officers and 110 men. Failed to reach establishment while on Isle of Wight and disbanded in early 1797, its recruits incorporated into Waldstein's (qv) Regiment.

Wood Several émigré officers' commissions to 'Colonel Wood's Regiment' or 'Wood's Legion' were granted in mid-1795. Some few elements may have existed, apparently in Germany, into 1796, but a unit could not be formed. An illustration of the 'Régiment de Houd' shows a soldier wearing an elaborate red uniform faced black and trimmed with yellow piping and cords.

Wurtemberg German regiment raised 1786 for colonial service with Dutch East India Company by Duke Charles Eugen of Wurtemberg. Arrived at Cape of Good Hope, 1788; thence to Ceylon, 1789, where it fought the British at Trincomalee, 1795, and at Colombo until surrender of 5.2.1796. Men of regiment then joined British service, and distinct 'Wirtemberg' company formed. This took part in capture of Dutch island of Ternate in Moluccas on 21 June; probably amalgamated into other units later. *Uniform:* In Dutch and probably early British service, blue coat faced with yellow; black leather dragoon-style helmet, the same as Meuron's Swiss.

York Hussars Raised from 13.5.1793, to consist of 600 men in three squadrons of two companies each; recruited in Germany but with some British officers including Col.A.H.Irwin. Distinguished itself in campaign in Holland; transferred to England, October 1795. Sailed for Haiti, March 1796, and in action from June. Many men perished from fever – less than 300 left by December, less than 240 by June 1797. Remnants of Rohan's and Hompesch's (qqv) drafted into regiment, and 170 replacements arrived early in 1798. Evacuated to Jamaica in August 1798; returned to England, October 1799. At Weymouth until transferred to West Cowes, Isle of Wight, June 1802, where disbanded on 24 July. *Uniform:* See illustration and Plate E.

York Rangers (also called Ramsay's York Chasseurs). Raised from 25.6.1793 by Capt.George W.Ramsay, initially with two companies each of four officers and 108 men – mostly Germans with some French-Irish émigré officers. Deployed in Flanders from August; fought with distinction near Menin in October; augmented to 600 men in three companies from November. Saw much action in Holland during 1794; withdrew with British forces into Hanover, January 1795, but reduced to 280. Recruited up to 732 all ranks in eight companies with an artillery detachment, and shipped to Portsmouth, January 1796. Embarked for West Indies, landed St.Lucia, fighting 'brigands' from May at Morne Fortuné; in June fighting Caribs on St.Vincent, where remained in garrison with a detachment on Dominica. Later transferred to St.Kitt's, with strength between 400 and 500 men. Ordered disbanded 24.8.1797; incorporated in October into 3rd Bn, 60th Foot on Tobago and Dominica. *Uniform:* See illustration and Plate B.

York Rangers (Ramsay's), 1793–96. Black cap with transverse brown fur and white metal star; blue jacket with yellow collar, cuffs and lapels, white metal buttons, yellow shoulder straps, blue wings with white lace; blue waistcoat braided white, blue pantaloons. (Anne S.K.Brown Military Collection, Brown University, Providence. Photo R.Chartrand)

SELECT BIBLIOGRAPHY

This compilation is largely based on two essential studies: C.T.Atkinson's pioneering series of articles on 'Foreign Troops in the British Army' published in the 1942–1944 issues of the *Journal of the Society for Army Historical Research*; and Vicomte de Grouvel's monumental *Les troupes de l'Émigration française*, Paris, 1957 (3 vols., of which Vol.1 concerns the British service). Archive documents consulted are in the British Public Records Office, Treasury and War Office (cited as PRO, TWO). Manuscripts by Charles Hamilton Smith are at the Houghton Library, Harvard University (C.H.Smith MS) and at the Victoria & Albert Museum, London. Other useful published studies were:

Beauchamp, Alphonse, *Histoire de la Guerre de Vendée et des Chouans*, Paris, 1807 (2 vols.)

Castries, Duke of, *La vie quotidienne des Émigrés*, Paris, 1965

Gerard, R., *Military Formations at the Cape 1652–1806*, Cape Town, 1953

Hugo, A., *France Militaire, Vol. 1*, Paris, 1833

Laws, M.E.S., 'Foreign Artillery Corps in the British Service', *Journal of the Royal Artillery, Vol.65 (1938–1939) and Vol.73 (1946)*

Lawson, Cecil C.P., *A History of the Uniforms of the British Army, Vol.4*, London, 1966

Martin, Jean-Clément, *Blancs et Bleus dans la Vendée déchirée*, Paris, 1986

Meuron's Swiss Regiment's grenadiers and light companies were in the 'forlorn hope' at the assault and capture of Seringapatam, India, on 4 May 1799. In this print after H. Singleton, the men, led by Captain Lardy with upraised sword, are shown at left. They wear the British service's red coatees with sky blue collar, cuffs and lapels, white turnbacks, pewter buttons, black round hat with bearskin crest and black plume tipped with red. The coatee without lapels and with white pointed buttonhole lace was adopted about 1800 for the men. Officers had long tailed coats and silver buttons and lace.

THE PLATES

PLATE A: LINE INFANTRY & ARTILLERY, HOLLAND & GERMANY 1794–1795

A1 Fusilier, Vioménil's Regiment
The regimental uniform was a red coatee with white collar, cuffs, turnbacks, piping and shoulder straps, pewter buttons stamped with the number '4'; a white waistcoat and breeches; black gaiters; and a black round hat with a bearskin crest and red turban and a white cockade, loop and plume. Officers had silver buttons and epaulettes.

A2 Officer, Autichamp's Regiment
The regiment wore a red coatee with sky blue collar, cuffs, turnbacks and shoulder straps, white piping, and pewter buttons stamped '3'; white waistcoat and breeches; black gaiters; a black round hat with a bearskin crest and red turban, and white cockade, loop and plume. Officers wore silver buttons and epaulettes on long-tailed coats, and wore bicorn hats with a white plume rather than round hats. Generally the officers of the émigré 'white cockade' regiments did not wear the crimson sash of British officers unless they served in line with British troops and/or were required to do so by the British commanding general.

A3 Grenadier, Broglie's Regiment
This regiment's red coatee was faced with violet at collar, cuffs, turnbacks and shoulder straps, with white piping and pewter buttons stamped '1'. Waistcoat and breeches were white, the gaiters black, and the headgear a black round hat with bearskin crest, red turban, and white cockade, loop and plume. Grenadiers like this moustachioed stalwart were distinguished by white epaulettes; and by a slightly higher hat with a small silver grenade badge on the turban, the front brim raised and edged with saw-tooth lace. Officers wore silver buttons and epaulettes.

A4 Gunner, Rotalier's French Emigrant Artillery
The gunners wore a blue coat with a scarlet collar, cuffs lapels and turnbacks, blue shoulder straps piped scarlet, yellow buttonhole loops and brass buttons. Waistcoat and breeches were likewise blue; a black bicorn hat displayed (officially) a red tuft and a white cockade with a black rosette at the centre. Bombardiers were distinguished by one yellow epaulette, corporals by two; company sergeants had gold lace, and staff sergeants also had gold epaulettes. Accoutrements were black, and weapons consisted of a brass-hilted hanger and a pistol hooked at the waistbelt. Drummers had the same uniform as gunners but were distinguished by wings; drivers wore coats without lapels. Wagoners had plain brown coats, waistcoats, breeches and gaiters; farriers, blacksmiths, saddlers, etc., wore brown with yellow epaulettes. Officers had gold buttons, epaulettes and lace and a white plume on the hat.

PLATE B: LIGHT INFANTRY, HOLLAND & GERMANY 1794–1795

B1 Officer, Waldstein's Light Infantry, 1795
The regiment wore a blue coatee with sky blue collar, cuffs

Jacques Cathelineau, one of the early leaders of the Royalist insurrection in the Vendée, was not a nobleman but a former wagoner and travelling salesman. Chosen as a leader on 12 June 1793, he was mortally wounded only a couple of weeks later, on 29 June, during an attack on Nantes; his death discouraged the rebel force and Nantes did not fall. Following the return of the Bourbons to the throne King Louis XVIII commissioned this and other portraits of Vendéan leaders. They are considered fairly accurate in spite of their romantic style, having been painted from eyewitness descriptions. Grey jacket, gold buttons, white waistcoat and sash, green-grey trousers, black cloak lined crimson. (Print after Girodet)

and lapels, yellow turnbacks, pointed white buttonhole lace, and pewter buttons; a white waistcoat, blue breeches, and black half-gaiters; and a Tarleton-style helmet with black fur crest, sky blue turban and white plume. Officers had silver buttons and lace. Accoutrements were white.

B2 Rifleman, York Rangers or Chasseurs (Ramsay's)
The black cap was furnished with brown fur and a white metal star; the blue jacket had yellow collar, shoulder straps, cuffs and lapels, white metal buttons, and blue wings with white lace. The waistcoat was white or blue braided white; and the men wore blue pantaloons. Gunners wore the same as the infantrymen but with red collar and lapels. Officers'

metal and lace was silver. Drummers had reversed colours – yellow jackets faced blue, piped white, with white turnbacks, two blue chevrons piped white on each lower sleeve; and a brown busby with a foxtail hanging at the left, but no plume.

B3 Rifleman, Hompesch's Chasseurs
This fine fighting corps wore green with scarlet facings, and a round hat with a black bearskin crest, scarlet turban and green plume.

B4 Rifleman, Lowenstein's Chasseurs
The uniform was a black round hat with a green plume; a blue-grey or dark sky blue coatee with green collar, cuffs, lapels and turnbacks and brass buttons; white (later green) breeches, black gaiters, and black accoutrements. They were armed with rifles provided with sword-bayonets.

BELOW **Charles Artus, Marquis de Bonchamps, was an experienced officer who had served in India. He joined the insurrection in the Vendée in March 1793; a good organiser, he soon led the best disciplined Royalist force in the west, and might have achieved much had he not been killed at the battle of Cholet on 17 October 1793. Grey jacket with gold buttons, white sash, dark trousers and cloak. Portrait of c.1817 after eyewitness descriptions. (Print after Girodet)**

ABOVE **The former naval lieutenant François Athanase Charette de la Contrie was living in the Marais area of the Vendée when a group of peasants sought his leadership. Charette initially fought in the Marais rather than joining the large chouan armies in 1793 but, because of his military skill and leadership qualities, he became the most powerful leader of the insurrection by the end of 1794. However, the numerous Republican armies invading the Vendée from all sides, and the failure of British and Émigré assistance, finally discouraged the rebels. Many laid down their arms, and Charette was captured and executed in February 1796. Blue hussar jacket with scarlet collar and cuffs, gold buttons and lace, grey trousers, white sash, black hat with gold lace and white plume. Portrait of c.1817, after eyewitness descriptions. (Print after Chasteignier)**

PLATE C: CAVALRY, HOLLAND & GERMANY 1794–1795

C1 Trooper, Damas Legion Hussars
The hussar companies of this mixed regiment raised for Dutch service wore a sky blue dolman and breeches, black dolman collar and cuffs, ash grey pelisse with black fur trim, mixed black-and-white cords and lace and pewter buttons. The barrel sash was crimson and white, the visorless shako

Chouan chief and volunteer, with a cannon drawn by bullocks; the Vendéan armies had up to 200 artillery pieces but lacked experienced gunners, powder, and an efficient train to move them quickly. Many were abandoned after bogging down on muddy ground. In March and April 1793 the rebels adopted the red emblem of the Sacred Heart on a white square, worn on the breast. According to the memoirs of the Marquise de la Rochejaquelin, the 'Vendéans had no military cockade; many stuck scraps of white or green stuff in their hats, others paper or leaves, and some nothing at all.' Some chiefs added white sashes, armbands, cockades, and even a white plume to their civilian clothes, but often 'there was nothing to distinguish the officers from the men except that they were better equipped.' (Print after Sarauge)

black with white lace and cords and black plume; the sky blue sabretache was edged white, with a crowned 'GR'. Officers had silver buttons and cords, crimson and silver sashes, and fox fur trim to the pelisse.

C2 Trooper, 2nd Regiment, Rohan Hussars
The regimental uniform was a white dolman with scarlet collar and cuffs, a scarlet pelisse edged with black fur, brass buttons and yellow cords; scarlet breeches trimmed yellow and Hessian boots edged yellow; and a visorless black shako with white plume and yellow cords. The sabretache was scarlet trimmed with yellow, as were the housings, and in the field white sheepskin saddle covers were used. Officers had gold buttons, cords and lace.

C3 Gunner, Salm-Kirburg Horse Artillery This unit was attached to the hussars but their dress was only partly of light cavalry style. They wore a grey coatee faced with black (or grey) at collar, cuffs, half-lapels (with four buttons each) and turnbacks; black shoulder straps edged white, and pewter buttons. They had a grey waistcoat, and grey hussar-style breeches trimmed with black, black hussar boots edged black; and a black round hat with bearskin crest, scarlet turban and white plume. They were armed with both sabre and carbine, and had black accoutrements. Officers wore silver buttons, cords and lace.

PLATE D: QUIBERON, 1795

D1 Fusilier, Hector's Royal Marine
These former sailors of the French Royal navy wore a red coatee with iron grey collar, cuffs, turnbacks and shoulder straps, white piping and pewter buttons stamped '2', over a white waistcoat and breeches with black gaiters. The black round hat was furnished with a red turban and white cockade, loop and plume. Officers had gold buttons,

epaulettes and belt-plates; the men's oval brass belt-plates bore the legend 'Hector' above a fleur-de-lis.

D2 Officer, Salm-Kirburg Light Infantry
Only 18 members of this unit escaped from Quiberon at the end of this catastrophic campaign, to be absorbed by the Loyal Emigrant regiment. Officers wore a scarlet coatee with scarlet collar, black cuffs and turnbacks, silver lace at sleeve buttonholes and silver buttons. See illustration elsewhere in this book for their men's dress.

D3 Fusilier, Breton Company, Loyal Emigrant
Raised locally after the landing and fighting with the rebel chouans of the Vendée from 1795 until at least the end of 1799, the company wore the wide-brimmed Breton hat rather than uniform headgear.

D4 The Duc de Choiseul
The duke was the commander of this ill-fated expedition. Having lost his baggage, he wore a campaign version of the uniform of the Salm Hussars – featuring a buff coatee with red collar and silver lace – lent to him by officers of the regiment.

PLATE E: HAITI, 1795–1798

E1 Officer, Uhlans Britanniques (Bouillé's), 1796
The first uniform worn by the Uhlans was a braided jacket and a square-topped czapka lancer cap, as illustrated – and note rear view in detail 1A. A new uniform was to be in wear by 1 March 1796; this consisted of a red coatee with green collar, pointed cuffs, lapels with seven brass buttons, turnbacks, and Polish-style piping on the back and rear sleeve seams; on a dress version of the coatee yellow lace edged the collar, cuffs, lapels and pocket flaps and square-

RIGHT **Private, 5th (Rifle) Battalion, 60th Foot, c.1797–1802. This battalion was really a German unit within the British infantry, having been formed in December 1797 on Barbados largely with men from Loewenstein's Chasseurs and Fusiliers. It was the first battalion on the British establishment to be armed with rifles, a weapon familiar to many of its initially German soldiers. Its uniform was quite distinct in colour and style from the standard red coat and bicorn: a green coatee with scarlet collar, pointed cuffs and piping, black and scarlet padded wings, and pewter buttons; medium blue tight pantaloons, black half-gaiters edged with red; a black shako with white metal bugle horn badge and green plume; black accoutrements, brass belt plate. (P.W.Reynolds after C.H.Smith)**

ended loops were applied to the lapels, but the everyday uniform was unlaced. The brass buttons were stamped 'HB' under a count's coronet (for the French phonetic version of the name, Hulans Britanniques). A white waistcoat was laced and corded yellow, and green breeches had yellow lace trefoils on the thighs; the lancer cap was as before. Officers had gold buttons, lace, cords and epaulettes.

E2 Fusilier, Gendarmes Royaux Anglais, c.1795

The infantry coatee was scarlet including the white-piped collar, cuffs and lapels, with white turnbacks, and white metal buttons stamped with the Royal arms – and note rear view in detail 2A; a black stock was worn with a short white waistcoat, white linen trousers, black shoes 'of the strongest sort' with leather laces, and a grey round hat with black cockade and plume. The uniform of the artillery was the same except for blue cuffs and lapels. The uniform of the cavalry differed only in the hat plume, decribed as 'black and red', and hussar boots instead of shoes (PRO, WO 6/5).

E3 Trooper, York Hussars, 1796–1798

Even on the march in the Mirebalais area of tropical Haiti in June 1797 the York and the Hompesch hussars wore their traditional uniforms, which in such a country presented 'a most singular & at the same time charming sight'. The regimental uniform of the York Hussars was a red dolman with green cuffs and collar, green pelisse with black (later white) fur trim, pewter buttons, white cords, crimson and yellow

sash, red breeches, and black mirleton cap with white cord and plume – although there were many variations. Officers wore silver buttons, cords and lace. Undress consisted of a green round jacket with red pointed cuffs and collar edged white, green shoulder straps and pocket flaps piped white, and 15 pewter buttons in front; white linen pantaloons with buttons on the sides, and a green forage cap trimmed white. (*The Haitian Journal of Lieutenant Howard, York Hussars, 1796–1798*, ed. R.N.Buckley, Knoxville, 1985)

PLATE F: THE EASTERN CARIBBEAN, 1796–1797

F1 Rifleman, Royal York Fusiliers (Hardy's)

C.Hamilton Smith sketched a rifleman in the West Indies wearing a green coatee with scarlet collar, cuffs and turnbacks piped white, black lapels piped scarlet, white-tufted wings, and pewter buttons; white waistcoat, green trousers, black half-gaiters; a black round hat with bearskin crest, red turban and green plume, and black accoutrements.

BELOW **Lieutenant J.A.Wolff, 5th Bn, 60th Foot, c.1797–1802. Many officers of the battalion were German, and they adopted a distinctly hussar style of uniform: green dolman and breeches, scarlet collar and cuffs, black cords, silver buttons, wings and lace at collar and cuffs; black Tarleton-style helmet with fur crest, green turban with silver chains, and green plume; black belt with silver badge, whistle and chain; crimson sash. (P.W.Reynolds after portrait)**

LEFT Private, Rifle Company, 6th Bn, 60th Foot, 1799–1800. The 6th Bn was raised in August 1799 with German recruits on the Isle of Wight. In 1800 it was sent to Jamaica, where it remained in garrison until November 1817; it then returned to Portsmouth to be disbanded in February 1818. The uniform of the rifle company was an all-green jacket edged with red piping including the cuffs and collar, and pewter buttons; white pantaloons confined by short black gaiters with green edging and tassels; a shako with a white metal bugle horn badge, green cords and plume. Accoutrements were light brown, including a waistbelt with an S-clasp, and a black powder horn cord. (P.W.Reynolds after C.H.Smith)

F2 Fusilier, Royal-Étranger

Another Charles Hamilton Smith sketch made in the West Indies shows Royal-Étranger wearing coatees with lapels but without lace, and round hats. The drawing is uncoloured but the uniform colours were probably sky blue coatee with red collar, black lapels and cuffs, white turnbacks and brass buttons; white waistcoat, and sky blue breeches.

F3 Rifleman, Lowenstein's Chasseurs

From the same series of Smith sketches: he shows a dark grey or black round hat with an up-turned brim edged green; a light grey-blue coatee and matching breeches, with green collar, cuffs, turnbacks, epaulettes and piping, and black gaiters. Some of his figures of this unit have no lapels and black crossbelts. Officers wore gold buttons and epaulettes.

PLATE G: MALTA & EGYPT, 1799–1802

G1 Fusilier, Corsican Rangers; Egypt, 1801

Vicomte Grouvel described a watercolour apparently dating from the Egyptian campaign showing a Corsican Ranger in a green single-breasted coatee, white-piped black collar, cuffs and shoulder straps (ending in white tufting); white lace loops on the cuffs only, and pewter buttons; grey breeches, black half-gaiters; and a black cylindrical shako with white metal bugle horn and green plume. The corps was allowed the sphinx badge on its buttons following this campaign, but probably disbanded before they could be made. The Rangers were armed with musket, bayonet and brass-hilted hanger, and had black accoutrements.

G2 Fusilier, Wateville's Swiss Regiment; Malta and Egypt, 1801–1802

According to Col.Louis de Watteville's journal, the 'regimental dress at that period (1801–1802) was a green coat, black collar and facings (e.g. cuffs). The arms and accoutrements were the same as they had been in Germany.' This uniform was generally similar to that of Bachmann's or Rovéréa's. (Journal of Louis de Watteville, Vol.1, copy at National Archives of Canada, MG24, F96)

G3 Officer, Roll's Swiss Regiment; Egypt, 1801

Officers of Baron de Roll's regiment had silver buttons, lace and piping. In Egypt they were sketched wearing plain regimental scarlet faced sky blue with silver buttons and two lace loops at the cuffs and collar, with wide-brimmed round hats.

G4 Trooper, Hompesch's Mounted Rifles

The corps wore a green coatee with scarlet collar, pointed cuffs, half-lapels, turnbacks and shoulder straps, and brass buttons; scarlet breeches and black boots; a scarlet shako with brass plate, black turban and cockade, and white plume with red base. Green housings were edged scarlet. Armed with sabre and rifle, the unit wore black accoutrements; and officers wore gold buttons and epaulettes.

PLATE H: PORTUGAL, 1797–1802

H1 Sergeant, Maltese (or Franco-Maltese) Artillery Company, 1797–1798

Based on a sketch taken in Portugal which appears to show an NCO. The blue coatee has a scarlet collar, cuffs and lapels, silver lace edging the collar and lapels and green piping edging the cuffs; white turnbacks; white flaming bomb badge on right sleeve, silver shoulder straps edged red, and white metal buttons. The waistcoat is white, the breeches blue, and black half-gaiters are edged with green lace, as is the round hat, which is furnished with a green turban and plume.

H2 Grenadier, Castries' Infantry Regiment

From 1797 the regiment wore a red coatee with light green collar, cuffs, lapels with seven buttons, turnbacks and shoulder straps, white lace edging the facings and white loops, with pewter buttons stamped with three fleurs-de-lis; white waistcoat and breeches, black gaiters; a black round hat with a bearskin crest and a red turban with white lace stripes, white cockade and plume – and note grenadier badges on turban and cockade. The hat was replaced by the stovepipe shako from 1800; its brass plate was stamped with the royal arms of France with 'Castrie's' above and 'Regiment' below. The Noble Chasseurs were to have the distinctions of sergeants for all. Officers wore silver buttons and epaulettes.

H3 Fusilier, Loyal Emigrant Infantry Regiment

From 1797, red coatee with yellow collar, cuffs, lapels and shoulder straps; white turnbacks; white square-ended lace loops with a blue line set in pairs, and pewter buttons; white waistcoat and breeches, black half-gaiters; round hat turned up at the left with white lace and band, black cockade, white plume. Chasseurs wore the same as fusiliers but with green hat lace, band and plume, white shoulder straps and wings edged yellow, and a red waistcoat with buttonholes trimmed with regimental lace.

H4 Fusilier, Mortemart's Infantry Regiment, 1801–1802

In 1798 a new uniform was distributed in Portugal: red coatee, black collar and cuffs (with two loops on the cuff and two above), lapels and shoulder straps; white turnbacks; white square-ended buttonhole loops, and pewter buttons stamped with three fleurs-de-lis. This was worn with a white waistcoat and breeches, black gaiters, and a black round hat with bearskin crest and red turban, white cockade with black centre, white loop and plume for fusiliers; grenadiers had white shoulder straps piped black, a small white metal grenade in front of the hat turban and on the cockade and a white-tipped red plume. Chasseurs had white shoulder straps piped black and a white-tipped green plume. From 1800 the new British stovepipe shako was adopted, its brass plate stamped with the Royal arms of France at the centre with 'Mortemart's' above and 'Regiment' below. The Chasseur Nobles Company had the same uniform but with the distinctions of sergeants for all. Officers had silver buttons, lace and epaulettes.

Officer's gilt shoulder belt plate attributed to Mortemart's Regiment, c.1794–1802.
It bears the inscription 'Régiment du Roi' (Regiment of the King) and the Roman numeral 'VII' engraved;
Mortemart's was the seventh in precedence of the émigré regiments. (Private Collection)